THE FAMILY IN THE
PRESENT SOCIAL ORDER

*The University of North Carolina Press, Chapel Hill, N. C.;
The Baker and Taylor Co., New York; Oxford University
Press, London; Maruzen-Kabushiki-Kaisha, Tokyo; Edward
Evans & Sons, Ltd., Shanghai.*

THE FAMILY IN THE PRESENT SOCIAL ORDER

A Study of Needs of American Families

BY

RUTH LINDQUIST

*Written and published with the coöperation
of the American Home Economics Association*

CHAPEL HILL
THE UNIVERSITY OF NORTH CAROLINA PRESS
1931

TO

A PASSING GENERATION OF MEN AND WOMEN WHO HAVE
PIONEERED WITH AFFECTION, FAITH, AND COURAGE IN THE
ADJUSTMENT OF FAMILY LIFE TO A NEW ORDER AND WHO
HAVE INSPIRED OTHERS FAR MORE THAN THEY KNOW
TO ENTER UPON THE DIRECTION OF FAMILY
LIFE WITH HIGH IDEALS AND A
CONTINUING FAITH

PREFACE

T HROUGH THE LENS of research in the physical and social sciences one views the modern home and parents as exceedingly important factors in the production of socially competent citizens. Such research has shown that the diet of child and adult increases or decreases the probability of good health; that conditions of housing affect the physical and social well-being of the individual; that the attitudes and objectives of the adults enhance the environment of the child or encourage prejudices which make adjustment difficult, if not impossible. These are but a few of the facts which science has already brought to our attention.

Education for marriage and parenthood is no longer an experiment; it is a reality, but curricula for such courses are yet to be perfected. The interrelation of the family and community has been recognized, though the types of aid which the home needs in order to function most successfully have had insufficient consideration. Research in some phases of home problems and family life has been begun. The relative importance of these projects in comparison with others that might be undertaken has not as yet been demonstrated.

If the way ahead is to be marked by steady progress rather than by mere change, there is need for a series of studies designed to discover present attitudes, outlooks, and techniques of different groups of actual homemakers. The results of such studies may well serve as a basis for building of curricula, for the development of agencies within the community, and for programs of research. Up to the present, attention has been centered almost entirely upon one type of home—the one which has failed or which has narrowly skirted failure—and consequently conclusions have dealt with what not to do in order that disasters might be avoided. This information is important, but not more important than that secured regarding successful homes. The experiences of able, thoughtful men and women who have surmounted difficulties and who desire completely functioning homes can add greatly to the factual basis. The present study is the first of what the writer hopes may come to be one in a series describing the types of homes and of family life on which our present civilization is being reared.

It is designed primarily for teachers and administrators in the field of education for marriage and parenthood, though it may have additional usefulness for students of social science and for those whose work and interests are directly related to present-day family life. A summary of the findings which seemed most useful to parents has already been published. In that portion of the study some of the means by which parents could promote more healthful and satisfying family life were presented; in the present summary the emphasis has been placed upon the helps which society can provide for the family.

The research reported in the following chapters has been sponsored by several groups and individuals. The Child Development and Parental Education Committee of the American Home Economics Association, with the coöperation of committees from Omicron Nu and Phi Upsilon Omicron, two national honorary fraternities in home economics, initiated the study and prepared the questionnaires used in it. The executive councils and the members of the two fraternities also participated by replying to the questionnaires or by securing heads of other families to do so. A grant from the American Home

Economics Association has helped to make possible the publication of the study. From each of these groups there has been only the most generous and helpful support wherever and whenever it was needed. To them and to the men and women who have provided the information on which this summary is based I shall continue to be deeply grateful.

Through the interest of the fellowship committee of the National Council of Parent Education, a Spelman Scholarship in Parental Education was granted for a year of study, and at the end of the time it was extended through a second year. The National Council has provided a part of the budget for clerical assistance and has shown a continuing interest in the project throughout the months in which it has been in progress. The staff of the Institute for Research in Social Science at the University of North Carolina has made available many facilities for expediting the compilation of the data. For the help received from each of these three groups I wish to record my gratitude.

Particularly do I wish to express my appreciation to Ernest R. Groves, who has been at all times the patient, thoughtful, and constructive adviser, and to Anna E. Richardson, who has contributed largely to the study from its initial organization to the final plans for publication. For Marion Talbot and Sophonisba Breckinridge, pioneers in the study of the modern household, who through their emphasis upon the interrelation of the individual family and the economic and social order have enabled many to catch glimpses of widened horizons, I can only express my admiration.

Finally I wish to make grateful acknowledgment of help received, in the actual preparation of the manuscript, from several of my friends and colleagues. These include Lillian Pearson Brinton, who has aided in compiling the data, Estelle R. Bean, who has assembled the replies, Mabel Bason, who has prepared the manuscript, and Anne Whitmer, who has edited it. In addition to this, I should like to express an especial appreciation of the kind and constructive criticism that I have received from Judith Clark. For permission to quote copyrighted material, acknowledgment is made to the National Bureau of Economic Research, Harper and Brothers, Harcourt, Brace and Company, The Macmillan Company, and Henry Holt and Company.

R. L.

Chapel Hill
December 20, 1930

CONTENTS

[xi]

LIST OF TABLES

LIST OF CHARTS

THE FAMILY IN THE
PRESENT SOCIAL ORDER

CHAPTER I

THE FAMILY IN A CHANGING ORDER

THE QUESTION as to the need for studies of the family and the wisdom of attempting to subject this particular type of institution to searching analyses is one which is often raised. For this reason the study reported in the succeeding chapters is prefaced by a summary of those changed and changing conditions in the economic and social order that make the modern home and family life different from any of its predecessors. It is the belief of the writer that only through an understanding of the changes in the material and non-material cultures can there be an approach to an understanding of the new adjustments which families find necessary. Those who are students of the economic and social order will doubtless find this introductory chapter merely a résumé of facts with which they have long been familiar. To them the writer suggests that they turn directly to the following chapter. There are others, however, who may find an orientation, such as this summary attempts to give, useful as a background for the study which is reported.

Variety in Family Patterns.—At the outset it is well to note the variety in family patterns which exists at the present time. While certain trends are apparent in perhaps a majority of the more than twenty-three million households reported in the 1920 census, there are many types which vary widely from each other in organization, in size, in purpose, and in the degree of adjustment to the age of which they are more or less a part. If a study of these differences in present-day families were made in detail, there is a probability that it would reveal the influence of cultural factors in the different stages of their development. For example, in the most remote areas of the country the type of family life approximates the older, self-sufficient pattern, while in urban sections there is a dependence upon a money income for the great majority of goods and services needed by the group. In the one case the industrial revolution has scarcely touched the organization in the mountain cabin; in the other it has given rise to an entirely new division of labor and to a great increase in the variety of economic goods and services which families consider essential.

Nor are the family patterns of today likely to be those of tomorrow. Changes continue to be written into the organization and the relationships of the household with signs only of an increase in number, rather than of any approach toward a static institution. The results of an investigation made today are likely to be totally different from those made a few years hence. In an attempt to survey the changes which, despite the fact that they have gone on outside the home, have yet influenced its structure and function, this continuing dynamic nature of society must be recognized.

Nature of Economic and Social Change.—In the following summary only those agents in the present economic and social order which appear to have been most largely responsible for ushering in new standards and changed relationships in family life are considered. They include the development of power machinery accompanied by the factory system and large-scale, specialized production; the use of machinery in agriculture, and production in rural areas for exchange rather than for use; the system of indirect distribution of economic goods; the acceptance of the profit motive in industry and commerce as the controlling one; the expansion of facilities for rapid and inexpensive communication and transportation; the system of free public education and the enduring belief in education as a remedy for many of the social ills; the changed position of women; the new status of the child; the freedom of movement from class to class as contrasted with a caste system; the emerging standards for health; new attitudes toward sex and marriage; the political and social philosophy of the nation with its emphasis upon individual rights and the laissez-faire doctrine, coupled with an increasing appreciation of the need for social control; the shift from religious orthodoxy to liberalism and unbelief among a larger percentage of the population; and, finally, the newer knowledge regarding both physical and mental health. In brief, through science and invention the old order has been replaced, and with the new order has come an American home life which has but few characteristics of the type from which it has developed. To these factors, if one would account for the rapidity and extent of some of the changes, must be added the effects of the World War.

Large-Scale Specialized Production.—Before the opening of the machine epoch, with its wage system and specialization of product, marriage was a distinct economic advantage for both sexes. The services of husband and wife resulted in the production, for the group, of the utilities required for health and comfort—utilities which were not otherwise available. The self-sufficient household raised and prepared its own food, made its own furnishings and clothing, and depended upon the members of the immediate family to supply diversions in the few leisure hours that remained after diverse productive processes had been completed. In a handicraft culture children were an advantage, for by their labors the supply of goods could be increased. While their contribution did not wholly pay for their "keep," they were less of a liability on the family balance sheet than they are in an era when a money economy, more costly planes of living, and compulsory school laws limit the amount that they can add by their services. Moreover, in adulthood they could be depended upon to care for their aged parents.

With the introduction and the use of expensive machinery for providing the population with many of the goods required for health and comfort, large-scale production became not only a possibility but a necessity. The use of water power served to increase further the needs for centralization of industry; as a result of these developments the growth of cities[1] and an increase in land values occurred. Since the cost of the new machinery helped to prevent individual ownership of the tools of production, there passed from the laborer a part of the control over his economic destiny. For the successful operation of the factory system the concentration of wealth seemed essential, with the result that the employing and employed classes emerged. During the years an increasingly large percentage of the population has become dependent upon the wage-system as a means of livelihood. Limited in his purchasing power by the contents of the wage envelope and by irregularity of employment, the worker has found home ownership less possible, for he has been unable to compete successfully with the

---

[1] The 1920 census shows 26 per cent of the population living in cities of 100,000 or above as compared with 15.4 per cent in 1890 and 18.8 per cent in 1900. From *Statistical Abstract of the Fourteenth Census*, p. 74.

capitalist in the purchase of land. For the latter, owner-ship has brought increased profits, while for the former it has provided family comforts and conveniences accompanied by sacrifices of other needs. Often it has lessened his freedom in bettering his economic condition. Thus, for the wage-earner and the salaried man ownership in a city has become less frequently the rule,[2] and control over the conditions under which they live has been more difficult.

This shift from domestic production by hand, with the family as a unit, to factory production by machines, with the workers gathered from many families, has been significant in decreasing isolation, in changing living conditions, and in substituting wages for home-made goods. It has been of importance, also, in creating a very great demand for unskilled and cheap labor. The exodus of the daughters of rural New England families to the textile mills in response to this demand may be regarded as the beginning of an increased economic independence for unmarried women in the United States and of a shift in the attitude regarding the place of women in the economic and social order. The encouragement of immigration from Europe and Canada in order to increase the supply of workers helped to populate the industrial centers with heterogeneous groups whose standards of living and attitudes regarding family life were the product of their different cultural heritages.

The factory system with the use of power machinery not only ushered in large-scale production and workers of different degrees of skill, but it promoted standardiza-

---

[2] Ownership has decreased from 47.8 per cent in 1890 to 45.6 per cent in 1920; ownership with encumbrances made up but 28 per cent of the total of owned homes in 1890, while by 1920 the ratio had increased to 38.3. From *Statistical Abstract of the Fourteenth Census*, p. 46.

tion, specialization, and an increase in the variety of economic goods available. Unrestricted competition necessitated the improvement of the product in each factory and either the guaranteeing of the qualities for which the buyer was willing to pay or the ability to persuade consumers that the product was one which was indispensable to them. Since machinery was designed for specific materials and processes, the manufacturer was limited to the production of a few articles and from the sale of these he must realize profits which were sufficient not only to maintain the industry but also to buy for himself and his family the goods and services which they regarded as essential. With the development of corporations the demand on the part of stockholders for dividends constitutes an additional item for which provision must be made. Further, the size of the dividend, together with the value of the stock, determines the amount of the capital which can be attracted.

In a culture where all of the people are dependent upon their earnings for specialized goods or services it is not strange that the pecuniary motive has become the dominant one, for without a margin in wages, salaries, or profits, commodities for production or use cannot be secured. When one recognizes the additional changes in the planes and the standards of living that have taken place in a generation and the increase in costs of living, the present fear of economic insecurity is the more readily interpreted.

Aside from the ability required to make an inelastic money income meet the needs of a growing family, there are new risks which accompany entire dependence upon earnings. The fear of unemployment is an ever-present one for a large number of families whose sources of income are wages or salaries, while the fear of bankruptcy for any one reason or for a combination of reasons becomes a dreaded spectre in the lives of those who rely on profits and dividends.

Individual security in an age of interdependence is exceedingly difficult to provide, while the effects of a lack of it are of graver significance than in the days of a self-sustaining household. Then the proximity of dwellings to those of friends and relatives generally insured sharing and neighborliness throughout the period of an emergency of whatever nature or degree of seriousness it might be. Now an impersonal system of furnishing credit in times of need demands references and securities which are analyzed in terms of economic soundness and profit. Humanitarianism is frequently regarded as out-of-line with good business policy. In addition, new and numerous hazards which accompany the present economic order make the satisfactory conduct of family life difficult, uncertain, and costly. To give but one example, the life span has increased from 49.24 years in 1901 to 57.32 years in 1926.[3] But the usefulness of men in industry declines rapidly after middle age has been reached.

Machinery in Agriculture.—Many of the characteristics of the modern industrial system apply also to agriculture, which has become increasingly mechanized, specialized, and commercialized. Even with diversification the farm furnishes only a small number of the products which are used in the home, and these, with the exception of garden produce, poultry, eggs, and milk, require the services of industry to prepare them for consumption. Produc-

---

[3] Louis I. Dublin, "The Economics of World Health," *Harper's Magazine*, CLIII, 738.

tion for use has been largely replaced by production for exchange. The rural family depends upon a money income only to a somewhat smaller extent, particularly in the case of food, than does the city family; and the number and extent of its purchases are determined by the prices which farm crops, animals, and produce bring, together with the supply and terms of credit available to the farmer.

The same changes in method that have occurred with the development of the industrial system are found in agriculture. In a machine age the man who attempts to till the soil after the manner of his grandfather loses out in the competitive struggle. Costly machinery is necessary, and the fact that an entire community of farmers needs the same equipment at approximately the same time, because of weather conditions and the change in seasons, means that coöperative use with shared costs is not practical. As a result the profits from the year's business cannot be used solely for the present and future needs of the household; in addition to that required for stock, seed, fertilizer, and feed a considerable part must be invested in buildings and equipment, in order to insure an income for the coming year. With the increasing amount of capital required for profitable production in a competitive money economy[4] and with an exhaustion of free and cheap lands, one can understand why farm ownership in the United States has decreased from 71.4 per cent in 1880 to 48.6 per cent in 1920, and why one finds a highly mobile rural population that is in striking contrast to the tradition of keeping the farm in the family through several generations.

[4] The average value per farm is given as $12,084 in the 1920 Census of Agriculture. This includes farm lands and buildings, live stock, farm machinery, tools and implements.

The degree to which modern agriculture differs from that of slightly more than half a century ago is indicated by Charles and Mary Beard in the following statement, which also shows the present position of the farmer in the price-fixing process of the machine age:

Throughout wide areas, the independent, self-sufficient farm unit of Lincoln's era had become a specialized concern producing for profit, forced to employ large capital in the form of machinery and fertilizers, compelled to compete with European agriculture on more equal terms and obliged to carry the weight of an increment in land values which had mounted with the years. With energetic members of the younger generation escaping to the cities to share in capitalist enterprise, with new racial stocks occupying ancestral homesteads, with a remorseless competition determining the prices of produce, with industrial capitalists and industrial workers compactly united to dictate terms on manufactured commodities, the economy and culture of historic American farming were crumbling into ruins.[5]

Indirect Distribution of Economic Goods.—Closely associated with the changes occasioned in family life by large-scale specialized production is the present system of indirect distribution of products. Producer and consumer are separated by countless middlemen who, though performing useful services, tend to conceal the real demand for goods and services, thus rendering production even more "planless." The risks involved in production and the losses that are the result of poor forecasting or changed business conditions necessitate prices which help to insure one against these uncertainties. Sound financing demands that as far as possible the profit and surplus items must be large enough to charge off heavy losses without risk of

[5] Charles and Mary Beard, *The Rise of American Civilization*, II, 277.

insolvency. Furthermore, the market structure requires a return that will insure a living for the hundreds who refine, sort, finish, store, pack, transport, or make other alterations in consumers' goods to the end that these commodities may be more attractive, more easily available, or more readily used.

The Profit Motive in Business.—The human weakness for conspicuous display is responsible for much of the fad and fashion in clothing, in household furnishings, in housing, in automobiles; the perennial appearance of "new models" of practically everything furnishes additional evidence of the situation. If families were isolated, the selling technique employed today would be less profitable, for people would be influenced less constantly by the buying habits of their friends and the extensive displays in shop windows. The so-called science of advertising, which utilizes the findings of both psychologists and economists—as someone has said—to persuade the consumer to purchase what he does not need and what he had not intended to buy, is another part of the mechanism that has made the process of choice a more difficult and costly one for the family. The present-day family not only buys many of the articles that were formerly produced in the home, but it purchases in addition many others that have come to be accepted as an essential part of the plane of living. In the majority of cases they reach the home only after a very round-about process of distribution, and their period of usefulness, for all but the staple articles, is limited by the change in style. One no longer wears a garment until it is worn out or keeps an article of furniture until it ceases to serve its purpose: the era of remodeling wearing apparel, too, has passed for many.

Closely related to the changes in the nature and the

number of goods used by the family is the departure of the modern family from the household routine of life that was accepted in the days preceding the industrial revolution. In much the same way that agriculture among primitive peoples passed from the women to the men, many of the time-honored occupations of wives and mothers have ceased to be regarded as a part of the household régime. For example, in agricultural areas where one or more cows were a part of the capital of the family, skimming milk and making butter were regarded as among the duties of the farmer's wife. Now even the ablest and the most widely recognized butter-makers of the community send their cream, separated by machinery rather than skimmed by hand, to the near-by creamery and buy butter with their cream checks. While there are those who complain about the price, most of them rejoice that they have been released from a time-consuming activity which required careful regulation of temperature and acidity in addition to skill of a high order and a goodly amount of patience. Bread-baking, garment-making, and canning, except for the period of the war, are other activities which are carried on increasingly outside the home. The era of ready-to-eat and ready-to-wear products has altered the woman's day both on the farm and in town and city. Labor-saving equipment and the transmission of power have also been highly important factors in this respect. While the day for many has not been shortened perceptibly, the hours are being used for different activities, and the new routine admits of a somewhat larger element of choice.

This decrease in the amount and kind of production carried on in the home is not without its problems for the family. Instead of two or more producers of a small number of essential goods, as was the case under the old system, the earnings of the husband, whether from his labor or his investments, are relied upon to furnish an increasing number of goods and services that have come to be accepted as the American standard. In other words, the new division of labor in the family has tended to shift the responsibility for the major part of production to the shoulders of the husband, while the wife's service has become that of directing the consumption by her selection of the goods and services offered through the shop, the market place, and the catalog. As has already been mentioned, the decrease in isolation that accompanied the new order has increased the apparent need for conformity and the social disapproval of variation from the generally accepted standards. Recurring periods of depression and prosperity in industry and agriculture have altered the regularity of the money income and the purchasing power of the dollar, thus causing fluctuations before which both income-earner and user are equally powerless.[6]

[6] In *The National Income and Its Purchasing Power* W. I. King makes the following statement regarding the effect of business cycles and periods of inflation and deflation upon the family; he compares the effect of these changes upon those dependent upon salaries and those supported by wages:

"The average annual earnings of the wage workers of the United States, when measured in terms of ability to buy consumers' goods show fluctuations much less marked than do those of the salaried employees. The common assumption, therefore, that the position of the salaried man is relatively secure while that of the wage worker is fraught with risk, needs considerable emendation before it can be accepted. The truth apparently is that the salaried employee is much less affected by the ups and downs of the business cycle than is the wage worker. The average wage worker, for example, suffered a considerable cut in purchasing power in 1914 and in 1921 while for the average salaried employees of the nation there was no tendency in either of these years toward a decline in earnings. On the other hand, salaried employees are much more exposed to the evil effect of inflation. . . . Salaries, however, being fixed largely by custom in terms of the money legal tender at the time, are depressed by every wave of inflation, and are later adjusted upward slowly during a period covering several years. On the other hand,

Rapid and Inexpensive Facilities for Communication and Transportation.—A continuing era of science and invention has brought about unparalleled developments in transportation and communication. The telephone, the rural free delivery system, radios, movies and talkies, hard surface roads, an automobile for every five people, the motor bus, the truck for long hauls, and the aeroplane have each helped to eliminate time and space. The effects of these innovations upon the isolation of families and the standardization of tastes and interests have already been pointed out. Markets, hitherto unknown, have been made accessible for everything from fruits and vegetables to household furnishings. No longer is the rural person identified by his queer clothes or by his lack of familiarity with current happenings. Programs that are broadcast to the most remote listener-in and news reels in village "theatres" keep one informed of the course of world events. The impetus that has been given to travel and the desire for leisure are clearly evident. If one spends a few nights in tourist camps or learns to recognize automobile license plates, he will soon begin to believe that all America is on wheels and that the children are given a chance from their earliest years to see something of the world. Indeed so traveled have even the poorest of the population become that the term "gasoline gipsies" is used by social workers to define a new type of problem which they face.

it is of course true that salaried workers gain during periods of deflation, for their salaries are not immediately reduced when commodity prices fall. Since 1923 the purchasing power of the average salary has risen materially more than has the purchasing power of the average wage. The increase between 1923 and 1927 being about 12½ per cent in the case of the average salaried employee as against 4 per cent in the case of the average wage worker."—Pp. 91-93.

Enlarged Educational Opportunities.—While the policy of providing free public education for all the children of all the people has been an accepted one in American thought for many decades, the amount of opportunity has varied considerably, and the rural child has been far less fortunate in the advantages afforded him than has the one reared in the city. The extent to which educational opportunities have changed in less than a century and the effect that they have had upon the methods of earning a livelihood have been brought out by the Beards.[1]

The development of the consolidated school and of legislation restricting child labor and making school attendance compulsory, together with the adoption of higher standards for the training of teachers and for their employment, has not only prolonged but improved the period of formal education for all, regardless of the attitudes, the background, or the wealth of the parents. The day of the supremacy of the three R's is passing, if it has not already gone, and today one finds curricula that aim to prepare the boy and girl in increasing measure for work, leisure, and associations. To the home this means that education for earning and homemaking has passed in large measure from the sphere of the parents, and that the school is coming to have a larger part in training for leisure and for the development of character. The more

[1] "When Lincoln was inaugurated there were only about one hundred public high schools in the country; by 1880 there were eight hundred; at the opening of the new century the figure had passed six thousand. . . . So thousands of youths, who in the older days or in contemporary societies elsewhere would have remained at the plow or the loom, squirmed their way into the middle class as lawyers, doctors, writers, teachers, and professional workers of every kind. Especially did girls take advantage of the new opportunities—flocking in increased numbers to high schools and colleges—in this fashion augmenting the independence of women and enlarging their empire over national culture."—*Op. cit.*, II, 468-70.

general acceptance of twelve or sixteen years in school as the minimum for sons and daughters has encouraged the postponement of marriage until after general and professional training has been completed and until economic security on a higher plane of living is made possible.

Most far-reaching in its effect upon the home is the decrease in sex discrimination in educational institutions of the present day. There is undoubtedly a greater willingness on the part of administrative officers, as well as of parents, for young women to enter professional schools, while the desire on the part of women to receive training for careers is indicated in the numbers to be found in schools of medicine, law, commerce, and nursing, not to mention those in schools of education and of social work. The number that are graduated each year from secretarial schools, from library science courses, and from business colleges cannot be estimated, but the fact that women are filling a great variety of positions is apparent to any observing person. The day has passed when teaching, clerking, and marriage were the three careers open to women. As the Beards have pointed out, "the multiplication and subdivision of trades, professions, arts, and crafts and the development of training schools of every kind enlarged the routes by which women could gain that coveted 'economic independence.' "[8] Because many of the schools are coeducational it is not strange that marriage has often lured women away before or shortly after a career was entered upon; however, in an increasing number of cases, they have found it possible and desirable to combine the two.

But educational opportunities are no longer limited to full-time day-school students in elementary school and col-

[8] *Ibid.*, II, 720-22.

lege. Continuation schools for workers, evening classes, extension and correspondence courses offer an unlimited array for the prospective student who has one or several hours each week or month in which to add to his store of knowledge, frequently at a time when he is more conscious of his needs than he was during the period when his chief business in life was getting an education. In addition there are many organizations which conduct study courses in which the content is determined by the interests of the group. Particularly does one find a variety of endeavor in the field of homemaking; programs range all the way from a local club program on tested recipes to a national course of study in child development. Home improvement projects of extension divisions, courses in nutrition, series of lectures by specialists on house planning and furnishings, papers on leisure time activities—these are but a few of the interests represented in the programs for adult education which provide information, inspiration, and increased confidence.

No complete discussion of educational opportunities can neglect a mention of the changes which have come with the development of modern methods of printing and power machinery. While the flood of literature which enables one "to educate himself through directed reading courses" may serve to engulf the person rather than to help him find his way to useful knowledge, one cannot complain that there is a lack of material. Books, magazines, bulletins, pamphlets, newspapers, and digests may be had for little or much money. Where public libraries are available, time only is required to take advantage of its resources. Syndicated articles frequently provide families with the gist of the newer knowledge in popular language. As one rural woman has said, "The postoffice is my greatest asset for through it I get a glimpse of the world beyond." To be unlettered and unread was once the fate of the many; today it is the fault of those who have chosen to use their hours for other things.

Changed Position of Woman.—There are many indications of the changed status of both unmarried and married women. Woman's entry into industry, the trades, and the professions increased from 14.7 per cent in 1870 to 24.0 per cent in 1920.[9] For married women the per cent employed in 1890 was 4.6 as compared with 9.0 in 1920.[10] In the professions alone there were 13.3 per cent of the women and girls engaged in all non-agricultural pursuits as compared with 6.4 per cent in 1870.[11] Whereas men of a generation ago dedicated books written by them to their wives, one finds today an increasing number of women who are co-authors with men. The sentiment that woman's place is in the home has at least been reinterpreted to mean that women need not marry in order to avoid an inferior social status, and that those who do marry need not perform all of the household activities, or even remain in the home throughout their waking hours, to prove their fitness as wives and mothers. The fact that many women enter upon marriage after they have been economically independent makes the process of adjustment for both the man and the woman very different from that which occurred when the route was from being a daughter in one home to being a wife in another.

There are other evidences of increasing freedom for women. The nineteenth amendment to the constitu-

[9] Joseph Hill, *Women in Gainful Occupations 1870-1920,* U. S. Census Monograph IX (1929), p. 19.

[10] *Ibid.,* p. 76.

[11] *Ibid.,* p. 41.

tion only ten years ago gave them the right of suffrage, a right which had been the subject of ardent pleas by feminists since before the war between the States. Legislative enactments in the several states have recognized the right of married women to collect their wages, to hold property in their own name, to have equal rights in the guardianship of their children, and, in some cases, to have separate domiciles. In theory at least, the patriarchal family is passing; however, joint partnerships in homemaking have emerged much more frequently in some types of American homes than in others. This is one of the points about which many of the generalizations made are not justified.

The Altered Status of the Child.—It is not alone the woman who has come to be regarded in the home as an individual with rights as well as duties. The earlier widely accepted theories that children must have work to keep them out of mischief and that the school of hard knocks and long hours was the best place for learning, have broken down to a greater or less degree depending upon the background of the parents. Even in cases where the privileges accorded to children by the parents are few, the demands and the behavior of children in neighboring families are infectious in their nature. The new freedom and leisure of youth, coupled with the refusal to recognize the older controls, present new difficulties and challenges both in and beyond the home.

Standards for Health.—The findings of science have brought to bear upon the family new standards for health. Whereas many epidemics had been regarded as plagues for which there was little help, a knowledge of the causes of specific diseases, the methods of preventing them, and the recognition of the costs of illness have gone far to-

ward an improvement in general well-being. The emphasis upon public health, the responsibility of the community, and the development of facilities for diagnosis
and treatment in rural as well as in urban areas have
made the interruptions which illness brings less necessary.
In this field particularly the wisdom of social regulation
is coming to be recognized. More recently the developing science of psychology and the work of scientists in
related fields are providing factual material[12] which gives
promise of revolutionizing the treatment of mental ills.
Attitudes toward Sex and Marriage.—Partly as a result of
the enlarged scientific knowledge has come a greatly
altered attitude regarding the place of sex in marriage
and in extra-marital relationships. The ban has been
lifted on sexual intercourse after marriage for purposes
other than procreation. The taboos are off. There is a
new freedom of expression in matters of sex. The decrees
of the Early Christian Church regarding moral and im-
moral practices are no longer so universally accepted.
Contraceptive measures, though not wholly efficacious,
provide a partial safeguard against unwanted parenthood.

In an era when machinery has replaced men, when
lands have become limited, and when children have
ceased to be financial assets, it is not surprising to discover
that families have shrunk in size. Not even the honorable
mention given by Theodore Roosevelt to the parents of
large families has been a sufficient incentive to present-day
parents to bear and rear the number of children that were
the rule in the families of their grandparents. Nor is a re-
version to the earlier tradition likely so long as the re-

[12] An article entitled "The Mind in the Breaking," by Dr. Haven Emerson
in *The Survey*, XVII, 366-70, refers to recent attitudes and developments in
this field.

sponsibility and the risks continue to be as great as they are. As a reaction against this very responsibility, one finds the companionate marriage which M. M. Knight of Barnard College has defined as a marriage contracted for the purpose of a legalized intimate comradeship of a man and a woman without the obligations of parenthood.

The increasing ease and frequency with which divorces have been secured in the past quarter of a century—from one in 12.5 marriages in 1900 to one in six in 1928—points to a new attitude toward the Biblical injunction, "What, therefore, God hath joined together, let not man put asunder." Although the *desire* for freedom in an earlier generation may not be adequately interpreted merely by the difference in the rates of divorce, the belief that marriages are made in Heaven is probably also less generally accepted. Desertion—"the poor man's divorce"—is but another evidence of the temporary nature of modern family ties. The breaking down of the earlier community of interests when the family was a self-sufficient unit, the decreased dependence of women upon marriage, and the unwillingness of child and adult to put up with discord or injustice help to explain the present situation.

American Political and Social Philosophy.—To the effect of the belief in individual rights and the freedom of contract reference has already been made. Individualism in many areas is still so uppermost that a minority is powerless to affect the social thought of the group. Whether the matter be that of marriage legislation or of vaccination for contagious diseases, both intelligent and ignorant men and women are prone to regard any movement which touches marriage and the home as an infringement of their personal and inalienable rights. The idea that the family is an institution affecting the social welfare in a most direct way and that marriage is therefore a civil contract, in addition to being a personal one, is snail-like in the slowness with which it gains ground.

Attitudes toward Orthodox Religion.—Finally, a profound influence upon family life—particularly upon the development of individuals—is the shift that is taking place from religious orthodoxy to liberalism and unbelief. The old restraining authority of the church has begun to lose its hold on individual conduct. While many new fears have developed, that of eternal punishment has diminished. With the old moorings gone for many and no new social controls recognized by them to any considerable degree, it is not strange that charting of life courses for child and adult is a difficult process. Transitory desires of the individual are likely to be the aim, with a large measure of self-control, consideration for others, and perspective no longer accepted as desirable.

Summary.—With the institution of the family, which is the product of a modern age yet shaped by the beliefs and attitudes of preceding generations, each person, whether in the rôle of member, educator, or adviser, is associated. An understanding of its present form and of the many variations in pattern that exist is desirable, if one would avoid the half-truths of self-declared prophets of a new and better order. The degree to which the developing industrial order, the findings of science, and the political and social philosophy of the United States have caused the homes of the present generation and the relationships within them to be what they are has been pointed out in the preceding pages. The likelihood that a dynamic society will create still other changes has been suggested. In the light of these changes research into the attitudes, the conditions, and the problems of homemakers and parents, in addition to a knowledge of the institutions which most directly affect the family, is desirable.

CHAPTER II

A DESCRIPTION OF A SELECTED GROUP OF FAMILIES

There is a tendency to use "the American home" as a blanket term in writings and discussions pertaining to the family. This usage implies the existence of a single type of home—one with like characteristics—which may be found in any section of the country. To know one group, then, would mean knowing all homes. In the preceding chapter the fallacy of such a generalization has been suggested. Aside from the fact that the relationships of the members grow out of monogamic marriage and that they are usually based upon affection, there are few distinguishing marks that apply equally to all.

On the other hand, there are countless examples of wide variations from a universal pattern. Marriage no longer necessarily implies the bearing of children, and in homes where there are offspring the period for which the parents assume the entire responsibility for the nurture and support of their young differs in length. Until comparatively recent years the modern home was one in which the male members, particularly the husband, brought in the money income. Today one in every eleven married women[1] is an earner. The wide range in the conditions under which families live alters the organization of home life at many points. Undoubtedly the degree of education of the parents determines in some measure the standard of living which seems essential for well-being. Because of the many and diverse types of patterns of home life within the United States, descriptions

[1] Joseph Hill, *Women in Gainful Occupations 1870-1920*, U. S. Census Monograph IX, p. 75.

[25]

of selected groups must constitute a first step in interpreting the needs and the goals of present-day families. A composite picture has the disadvantage of concealing many of the characteristics and aspects which are of interest and importance in understanding the different types of families. It shows the usual or the "average" only.

In the study which is reported in these chapters the 306 families who helped to make it possible were chosen in two ways. At the outset the alumnae members of two national profesional fraternities in the field of home economics, Omicron Nu and Phi Upsilon Omicron, were asked to furnish information on their own homes if they were married and had one or more children. This method resulted in reports from homes in which the women were graduates of a four-year college course in home economics. The coöperation of the entire alumnae and honorary membership of the two fraternities was encouraged by asking those who were unmarried and those who were married, but without children, to have the homemaker of their acquaintance whom they considered "most successful" furnish information. In this second group were college graduates of courses in home economics, graduates with other majors, and those who had less than a college degree.

In Table I is found a classification of the families according to the type and amount of formal education of the homemakers.

Seventy-five per cent of the women had received their degrees upon completion of a major in home economics; 8 per cent were graduates with a major in some other field; and 17 per cent had had less than a college degree. Of the total number 10 per cent had degrees of master of arts, master of science, or doctor of philosophy.

TABLE I

THE AMOUNT AND TYPE OF FORMAL EDUCATION OF THE MEN AND WOMEN
IN THE FAMILIES COÖPERATING

	Men		Women		Both Sexes	
	No.	Per Cent	No.	Per Cent	No.	Per Cent
College Graduates............	(210)	(68.6)	(253)	(82.7)	463	75.6*
Home Economics..........	...	....	228	74.5	(228)	(37.2)
Other Courses............	210	68.6	25	8.2	(235)	(38.4)
Not College Graduates†........						
High School Graduates.....	71	23.2	48	15.7	119	19.4
Less than 12th Grade......	25	8.2	5	1.6	30	5.0
Total...............	306	100.0	306	100.0	612	100.0

* In 57 per cent of the homes both husband and wife were college graduates; 23 per cent of the men and 10 per cent of the women had advanced degrees.
† Ten per cent of these had some work beyond high school.

Of the total number of men 68.6 per cent had college degrees, and very nearly one-fourth of the entire group among the men had advanced degrees. A larger per cent of the husbands—31.4 per cent as compared with 17.3 per cent for the women—had had less than college degrees, and practically one in ten of these had not graduated from high school.

The selection of the coöperating families largely on the basis of the type of education of the wife resulted in a bulking of other characteristics which, though they held true for the group studied, would not be typical of a random sample of families taken from the nation at large. In Table II the large percentage of both sexes under forty years of age is seen. For men and women there are 83.1 per cent; for women alone the figure is 87.7 per cent, and for men alone it is 77 per cent.

As one would expect, the number of years since marriage for a group which is relatively young in years in-

TABLE II

AGES OF THE MEN AND WOMEN IN THE FAMILIES COÖPERATING

Ages	Men		Women		Both Sexes	
	No.	Per Cent	No.	Per Cent	No.	Per Cent
19–24	...	....	1	.3	1	.2
25–29	28	9.2	63	20.5	91	14.9
30–34	104	33.9	122	39.8	226	37.0
35–39	107	34.9	83	27.1	190	31.0
40–44	37	12.1	24	8.0	61	10.0
45–49	19	6.3	10	3.3	29	4.7
50–54	6	2.0	2	.7	8	1.2
55–59	3	1.0	1	.3	4	.6
60 and over	1	.3	...	....	1	.2
Not given	1	.3	...	....	1	.2
Total	306	100.0	306	100.0	612	100.0

dicates that for the most part these are not long established families. The percentages shown in Table III indicate that fully half of the homes have been established less than eight years, and that only 8 per cent were founded fifteen or more years ago.

TABLE III

NUMBER OF YEARS SINCE MARRIAGE

No. of Years	No. of Families	Per Cent of Families
Under 2	7	2.2
2–4	56	18.3
5–7	94	30.7
8–9	53	17.4
10–14	72	23.5
15–19	15	5.0
20–24	6	2.0
Over 25	2	.6
Not given	1	.3
Total	306	100.0

In the group studied approximately one-third had one child; another third had two children; and a slightly smaller group had three or more. The exact percentages are found in Table IV.

TABLE IV

NUMBER OF CHILDREN PER FAMILY

No. of Children	No. of Families	Per Cent of Families
1...................................	115	37.5
2...................................	100	32.5
3...................................	71	23.3
4 or more...........................	20	6.7
Total.........................	306	100.0

The fact that somewhat more than half of the total number of children were under school age gave evidence that the families were in the process of growth rather than in the stage of disintegration which comes when the responsibilities of adulthood are approached by all of the individual members of the group. The percentages in the different age groups appear in Table V.

TABLE V

AGES OF THE CHILDREN IN FAMILIES

Age Groups	No. of Families	Per Cent of Families
Under 2 years........................	121	19.7
2– 5 years...........................	251	41.0
6– 9 years...........................	146	23.8
10–14 years..........................	72	11.7
15–19 years..........................	17	2.7
20–24 years..........................	6	1.1
Total.........................	613	100.0

In the range of occupations this selected group of families is somewhat representative of a random sample, but in the proportions of men in the skilled, unskilled, and professional classes there is a wide variation from such a sample. Those in teaching and in the other professions greatly outnumber those in the trades—a fact which can be explained by the exceptional educational opportunities and training which 68.6 per cent of the men have had.

The statement that the provision of the money income is no longer entirely delegated to the male members, and particularly to the husbands, of the households has already been made. In this group, in which eighty-two out of each hundred women were college graduates, there were ten women who were carrying full-time positions in addition to that of homemaking. Forty-four—15 per cent—reported part-time work, and several indicated a desire to find work which would bring in regular earnings. A few were emphatic in their unwillingness to assume an added responsibility because they felt it would interfere with homemaking in general or with the development of their children. As was true in the case of the occupations of the men, a wide variation in the types of work was indicated. Educational work, particularly teaching, however, was most frequently mentioned both by those who reported full-time and by those who reported part-time employment. Several were writers, and others were assistants in the husband's business.

It is chiefly in the size of the annual incomes that this selected group of families differs from the average. In Table VI the figures are presented. Whereas the average income in the United States for those gainfully employed is estimated at $1,920 for the year 1928,[2] only one in four

² W. I. King, *The National Income and Its Purchasing Power*, p. 87.

of this group who reported on this point had less than
$2,500 for the family. It is possible that the percentage
would be slightly larger if the 6.2 per cent who did not
report the amount had given the information requested.

TABLE VI

SIZES OF ANNUAL INCOMES

Income Groups	No. of Families	Per Cent of Families
Less than $1,800......................	4	1.2
$1,800–$2,500........................	72	23.5
2,500– 3,500........................	75	24.5
3,500– 5,000........................	86	28.2
5,000– 7,000........................	27	9.0
7,000–10,000........................	14	4.7
10,000 and over......................	9	2.7
Not given............................	19	6.2
Total..........................	306	100.0

In a separate study[3] of sixty-two rural families, which
was made in part from those coöperating in the present
study, one in every two families reported less than $2,500
annually. Data regarding the size of income earned by
one out of every eight of the rural group who received less
than $1,800 were lacking. Apparently the amount stated
by rural families referred to the gross cash income and
did not include either the value of the produce used by
the family or the operating costs of the farm business;
hence the figure for the total receipts is less accurate than
are those given for urban families.

The homes which are included in this study are located in rural areas, small towns, and in small and large
cities throughout the country. The South contributes

[3] Ruth Lindquist, *A Study of Home Management in Its Relation to Child
Development*, p. 4.

but few coöperating families; whereas the states of Ohio, Illinois, Kansas, Iowa, and Minnesota furnish the majority. The proportion of rural homes included is very much lower than that for the nation—only 10 per cent as compared with 25 per cent.

From a more detailed study of the three groups of women classified according to the nature and the amount of formal education which each has had (Table I) one observes that there are several points of difference among the families of which these women were members. Tables in Appendix I are the basis for the summary of the differences listed below:

1. The period of marriage for more than half of the women who majored in home economics and for one-third of those who majored in other departments is less than eight years. In the group made up of those without college degrees only 28 per cent have been married as short a period.

2. Sixty per cent of those who are not college graduates have been married ten years or more as compared with 48 per cent of those who are graduates with a major other than home economics and 22 per cent of those who majored in home economics.

3. Only 28 per cent of both groups of college graduates had more than two children; 39 per cent of those without college degrees had three or more children.

4. The size of the annual incomes is smaller for the group in which the woman was without a college degree and for the one in which she had a major in home economics. More than one-half of both of these groups had less than $3,500; 19 per cent of the non-graduate group and 14 per cent of the home economics trained group received $5,000 or more, as compared with 32 per cent of the group who had majored in a department other than home economics.

These differences are of importance and will be referred to in a later analysis of the helps and needs which wives and mothers have encountered.

In the foregoing pages there has been an attempt to summarize some of the more objective characteristics of the families that have been studied and to point out some of the differences that exist within the group, as well as to indicate the respects in which the group as a whole differs from a cross-section of the families of the United States. It is a consideration of the needs of this selected group that constitutes the major part of the following chapters. There is in addition, however, an attempt to set up some of the questions which seem relevant to other types of present-day families and to projects for research in home and family life.

CHAPTER III

SOME SOURCES OF FATIGUE, WORRY, AND FRICTION IN FAMILY LIFE

THE POINTS at which stress and strain occur in the intimate associations and the varied activities of family life afford useful data for those in the field of education for marriage and parenthood. There is need for a comprehensive study of the attitudes and reactions of adults and children in a representative sample of homes. In the present study the information available is concerned with no more than the sources of fatigue, worry, and friction which appear to wives and mothers; their statements, however, do throw into bold relief questions which might well form the subject of more intensive research both in a similar type of homes and in those which vary from this type.

Sources of Fatigue.—In the chart appearing on the opposite page will be found the sources of fatigue, worry, and friction which seem uppermost to the women in the 306 homes represented in this study. Fatigue of the mother is recorded far more frequently than either worry or friction, but it appears to bear a close relation to both of these. There are many individual comments to the effect that weariness of muscles or nerves increases the amount of friction and the tendency to worry. If fatigue is one of the signs of poor health, then the problem becomes a complicated one, a fact which is well brought out in the following statement by one of the women:

But, in spite of everything, I have long since reached the conclusion that a mother can do most anything (that is, of course, within reason) for her kiddies with a smile if she is

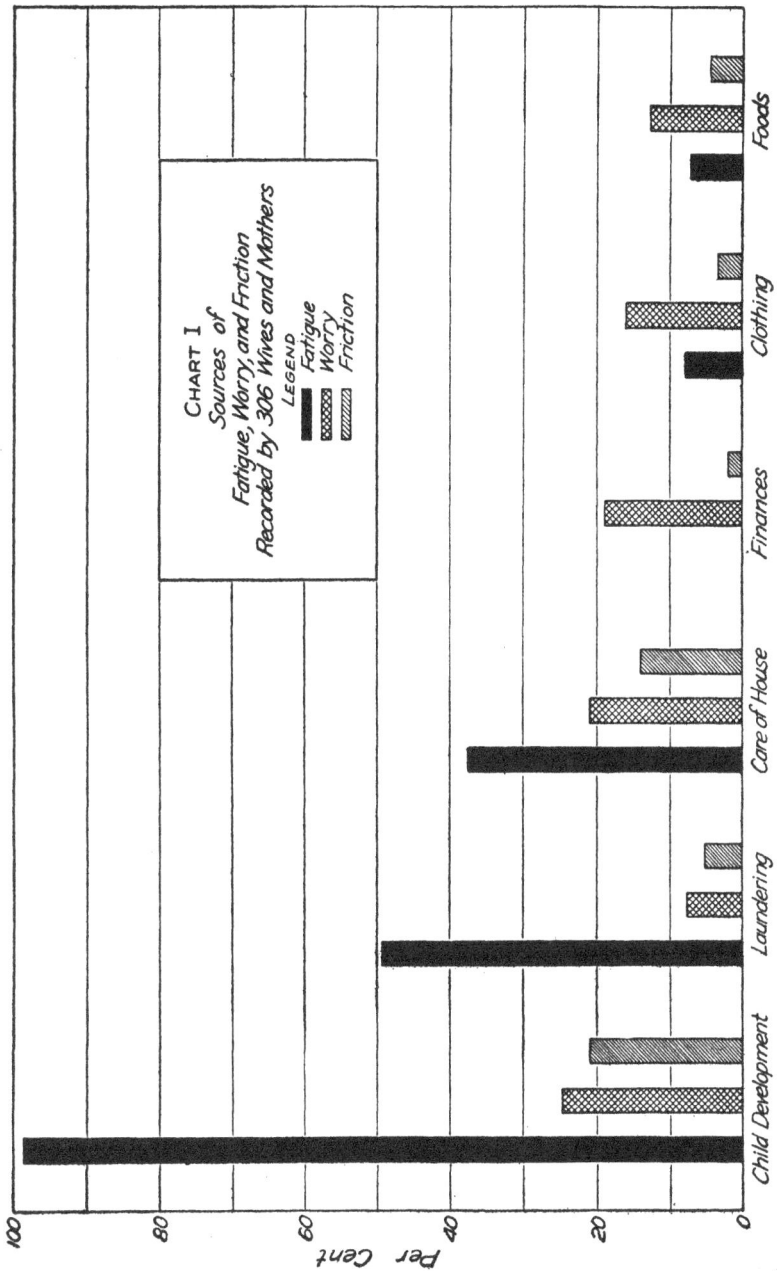

CHART I
Sources of
Fatigue, Worry, and Friction
Recorded by 306 Wives and Mothers

LEGEND

Fatigue
Worry
Friction

Per Cent

Child Development   Laundering   Care of House   Finances   Clothing   Foods

well. That's the backbone of the whole theory of home management, child training, and outside interests. It is all right to guide and direct, but if there is no strength left to carry out the plan, when once begun, it all fails.

The responsibility of caring for and training children is the one which occasions the most comments from these mothers. That there is a physical and nervous strain which taxes all but ten of the entire group is apparent. Thus it would seem that fatigue resulting from the direction of children throughout the process of growth cannot be attributed to any one set of factors, such as age, training, income, or attitude. One in every eight women indicates that endurance is highly important for the physical care of infants and young children. Bathing, lifting, and carrying infants are processes which several women mentioned specifically. The fact that one is always on call limits the completeness with which many relax. Lowered physical reserve following the period of childbearing makes the strain a doubly heavy one for some.

If there can be some time daily or weekly when young children are satisfactorily cared for by persons other than the mother, a new perspective and a new lease on life are gained. The refreshment and relaxation which "time out" affords enables these women to secure, or maintain, their poise and to evaluate affairs of the household much more wisely than they are able to do when they are constantly "on the job acting as philosopher, judge, and peacemaker." The strain that comes from living under the same roof with one's responsibilities is lessened when there is an opportunity for some freedom and individual relaxation. This is the advantage which many of those who are working outside the home see in employment for married women. There are several who add that the cultivation of extra-household interests makes wives and mothers more interesting and stimulating companions for their husbands and children, in addition to increasing the ease with which social contacts beyond the family are made.

Laundering ranks second as a source of fatigue. In comparison with the care and guidance of children, however, there are only half as many who report it.[1] Yet the extent to which it is regarded as a cause of weariness is seen in the accompanying chart. One in every two women in the group mentions one or all of the processes connected with keeping clothing and linens clean among the fatiguing ones for her. One in every five finds both washing and ironing tiring; one in every six mentions ironing specifically; and one in ten lists washing alone. When the amount of electrical appliances for laundering that are on hand in these homes is considered, it would seem that they have not of themselves solved the problem.

An analysis of the situations which exist in the families where women find these activities particularly fatiguing shows that it is the mothers of young children, without help, who become weary in the attempt to fit these activities into a week of constant, but often uncertain, demands. Possibly a lack of the skill which comes with repetition of the processes over a period of years, together with less willingness to accept this duty as one to be carried by the woman herself, accounts for the greater difficulty that young mothers have. The extra amount of laundering which must be done when there are young children and the greater frequency ne-

[1] The fact that the questionnaire included a separate question regarding the effect of the constant responsibility of children upon the mother may be in part responsible for this proportion and the others which are reported in succeeding paragraphs. For the form of the questions See Outline III in Appendix II.

cessitated by this no doubt explains in part the reason for fatigue.

The processes carried on in keeping the house clean and orderly are, in order of frequency, a third source of fatigue. Although seasonal cleaning is mentioned specifically by slightly less than one in ten, one in four finds that the sweeping, dusting, and mopping which must be done daily or weekly reduce the physical reserve. Particularly is this true in the homes where there are one or two young children and little or no available service either from the family or from paid workers. The degree to which the husband assumes responsibility in the home and his attitude toward the standards which his wife is attempting to maintain seem to be factors of considerable importance. The "everlasting picking-up" which is necessary if the home is to be kept presentable occasions both fatigue and friction.

Additional sources of fatigue are minor when compared in frequency with those mentioned above. Unfortunately any accurate comparison of the *amount* of fatigue occasioned by the various activities cannot be made until some measuring stick is devised which can be used successfully for the varying conditions under which homemakers work. Among the processes which are mentioned by smaller numbers the manifold duties of homemaking are recorded in one of every twelve replies. Sewing and mending, if they are kept done, tire some. The entertainment of guests and participation in outside activities are wearing for a few.

Dislike for particular tasks seems to bring on fatigue, whereas the activity which one enjoys, or the one which is easily completed, is rarely a cause. Those, for example, who find sewing difficult or picking-up monotonous record these as fatiguing. In this connection it is interesting to note that food preparation and meal planning, in which slightly less than eight out of ten of the women have had college training, is rarely listed as a reason for weariness. In the majority of instances where food is mentioned the home has been established only a few years and there is one young child who requires a considerable amount of the mother's time. Many of the group who find these activities tiring are those who have but little training in the principles and technique of food selection and preparation.

An additional factor which affects the degree of fatigue reported by these women is the size, the arrangement, and the conveniences of the dwelling, and the neighborhood in which they live. This is most clearly brought out in a study of the rural homes in which money is lacking for the improvement of the house. Particularly does the lack of modern conveniences complicate the day for the women who must do all of their own work in order that any margin over and above expenses can go back into the farm as a means of increasing future incomes. It is apparent that a lack of space and the practice of using one room for several purposes, such as is common in cities today, have disadvantages also, if considered from the standpoint of the one who cares for the house and from the standpoint of one who is trying to reduce the friction that grows out of a lack of privacy.

The amount and the efficiency of household equipment which women use help to shorten the day and increase the satisfactions that come from doing the everyday tasks. It is interesting, however, to find that the four pieces of equipment mentioned most frequently as those saving time and energy are the electric vacuum cleaner, the electric washer, the iron, and a motor for the sewing machine. In other words, three of these are being used for the processes which continue to occasion the greatest amount of fatigue. There is a desire on the part of practically all of these mothers to have their children grow up in homes equipped with as many of these labor-saving devices as possible in order that they may be relieved of the drudgery that is necessary without these helps.

Unquestionably a striving for perfection keeps many women from securing more relaxation and diversion. A standard of cleanliness and order that can be maintained only if *living* in the house is subordinated to keeping everything and everybody spic and span results in friction as well as in fatigue. This emphasis upon housewifery appears to grow out of the training which has been received in the home of one's childhood, the standards that have been set in college courses, the obligation that the woman feels to rest upon her in the community, or a combination of all three. In a few instances it seems to be a symptom of dissatisfaction with homemaking and associations in the family.

The length of the homemaker's day may be regarded as a fairly accurate index of the load which she is carrying, although the degree of skill, rather than the number of hours worked, determines achievement. This information does afford a basis for comparing the constancy of homemaking with other occupations and the amount of time that is available for outside interests and diversions. Unfortunately the present study is lacking in figures which have been carefully and completely set down. Where hours and minutes have been recorded they represent estimates for the most part and are probably less accurate than the results of actual time studies. Out of the entire group less than two in three gave information that seemed definite enough to incorporate in a statistical summary. Factors, such as the number in the family, the ages of the children, the size of the income, the amount of assistance which the mother had, the type of house, the number of conveniences, the amount and kind of equipment, the degree of skill, and the amount of work done outside the home by the woman, made for such wide variations within the small group that the results are of interest in suggesting further studies rather than as a basis from which conclusions may be drawn. From the figures which have been assembled[2] one finds that the average day for the mother is made up of the following parts:

	Daily	Weekly
Housekeeping and routine tasks......	7 hrs. 35 mins.	53 hrs. 5 mins.
Family life, including supervision of children.....................	2 hrs. 35 mins.	18 hrs. 5 mins.
Garden and outdoor activities........	10 mins.	1 hr. 10 mins.
Outside activities..................	40 mins.	4 hrs. 40 mins.
Total......................	11 hrs.	77 hrs.

For rural women the average spent in routine tasks is considerably higher—nine hours—and the amount used for outside activities is but a half-hour daily. The average for women in urban homes who have only one child is 7 hours, 18 minutes as compared with 6 hours, 54 minutes, used by the mother of four children in doing daily household tasks. If individual cases are studied, one finds a much greater variation. For example, one rural mother with two children spent 5 hours, 50 minutes and another with the same number in the group reported 14 hours, 11 minutes.

[2] L. P. Brinton, An Unpublished Study on Keeping Time. This is based upon the reports furnished by 184 of the 306 women who coöperated.

Some of the findings[3] show that in these homes there is a definite relation between income and the length of the day for families living in town and that there is a distinct shortening of it after the income reaches $3,500 annually.

In the rural home, on the contrary, a high gross income does not result in a shorter day for the extra funds are used for building up the farm business.

The presence or absence of a number of children, the income remaining constant, sends the length of the day to opposite extremes, varying, however, with the ages of the children.

There does not seem to be any great increase in the amount of help given nor the number of functions performed by the fathers in the home as the number of children increases. Neither does the father seem to help a great deal more when the income is low. The differences in the amount of help given seem to be due to the training in helpfulness that the man has had in his childhood home, his willingness and his aptitude in learning, his desire to be of assistance, and the free hours which he has.

The types of assistance most commonly used are those which lessen the amount of energy that women must spend on the fatiguing tasks—cleaning, laundering, and the care of children.

The figures derived from these estimates are not strikingly different from the much more comprehensive study of time records which has been made by the Bureau of Home Economics of the United States Department of Agriculture, and they seem to indicate that the averages are not too high:

[The records of more than 2,000 homemakers show that] five-sixths of these homemakers spent over 42 hours a week in their homemaking, more than half spent over 48 hours, and

[3] *Ibid.*

one-third spent over 56 hours. The average for all is slightly over 51 hours a week. . . . If we take this range of 42 to 56 hours as roughly marking the limits of what might be considered a full-time job in homemaking, exactly half of the homemakers will be found within this class, while one-third will be classed as overworked and only the remaining sixth as underworked. Judged by this group of housewives, homemaking is still for the majority a full-time job, and too much work is still a more frequent problem than too little.[4]

The nature of the activities which require the full-time services of the women who are homemakers bears out the findings of the present study:

The homemakers in the Bureau Study spent an average of only 2½ hours a week in purchasing, planning, and other management, and only 4½ hours in care of members of the family—in dressing and bathing children, in teaching, supervision, and other direct care. It is the routine housework— the provision of meals, the care of the house, the laundering and mending—that still requires the bulk of the homemaker's time. She is still predominantly a housekeeper, rather than a household manager.[5]

Sources of Worry.—There are several responsibilities which create worry or anxiety for the mothers in this group. Chief among them is the direction of the children in such a way that the qualities of character which are essential for a successful and satisfying personal life may be developed. Lack of understanding regarding child nature and of time to guide the child in his emotional and moral growth troubles one in every five women. Physical care appears to be managed by prac-

[4] Hildegarde Kneeland, "Is the Modern Housewife a Lady of Leisure?" *Survey Graphic*, LXII, 301.
[5] *Ibid.*, p. 302.

tically all of the group without this feeling of parental inadequacy. Lest the attitudes of the mothers on this point be unintentionally over-rated, it should be said that the degree of concern cannot be measured. It is possible that the returns should be interpreted as meaning that child guidance is the most perplexing problem which they face, but that it is not one by which they are overwhelmed. Further studies on this question are needed.

Although household processes appear less often as a source of anxiety or worry than they do as a source of fatigue, they are to be found in this group also. One out of every five worries about the care of the house. For several a lack of orderliness and difficulty in securing the coöperation of the members of the family in keeping their possessions in place is troubling. Finding time and patience to do the sewing and the mending regularly disturbs very nearly as many women as do financial matters but a difference in degree is noted in the replies. Whereas problems regarding clothing constitute a source of worry, finances are the problem which provokes the greatest anxiety. Planning the meals and the preparation of food are activities which cause worry for fewer than one in ten women. A slightly larger proportion regard the many duties of homemaker as a source of anxiety. A fear of illness accompanied by a depleted treasury and a permanent handicap is indicated by several.

Third in order of frequency among the causes of anxiety are financial problems. For the most part they center about the difficulties which arise from an income which seems inadequate for the standard of living that is desired. Methods of increasing the annual receipts and of using the earnings wisely cause concern and uncertainty. The desire to provide an education for the children and to lay aside enough money for the proverbial rainy day is recorded by many. Slightly more than one in every six seem unable to throw off the weight occasioned by financial matters. Differences of opinion on the part of the husband and wife regarding what constitutes wise use of the income complicate the problem.

When high ideals for the conduct of family life are held and there is a desire to attain them, it is not strange that shortcomings of individual members and little measurable progress cause anxiety for those who are responsible, in part at least, for the standards which have been set. Several refer to their own inadequacies as wives and mothers, and some seem overcome by the goals for which they are striving. Differences from their husbands in point of view and in temperament occasion disturbances which they would like to prevent. Misunderstandings and conflicts between parents and children are also sources of anxiety. Inability to use paid service effectively in the home troubles some women.

Sources of Friction.—In the attempt to make both ends meet and to carry her full share of the financial burden, the wife willingly serves as cook, housekeeper, laundress, hostess, buyer, and general manager. Later, as the children come and the pressure upon the income, which increases but gradually at best, is greater, she performs the same tasks for a larger group and assumes in addition those of seamstress, nurse, caretaker, and personnel director. It is the responsibility of being all things to one's family, not through a forty-eight-hour week or a fifty-week year, but on demand and with only occasional time off, that lowers the physical reserve of the woman and brings on friction between members. There is practically a unanimous agreement that much of the irritation and friction which occurs in the course of the week could be greatly reduced if mothers were relieved from the responsibility for young children with a fair degree of regularity either daily or weekly and without feeling that they were loafing on their jobs.

There is abundant evidence that a tired mother is a cross and impatient one. Relationships of parent and child often lack harmony as a result of the fatigue of one or both parents. The degree to which one woman who now has a family of grown children went when the children were young is quoted:

A mother needs relief if she is to keep well balanced. I was hardly ever relieved of my children when they were young and I was so *driven* that once I threw the carbolic acid in an outdoor privy vault lest I take it some day.

While this instance is undoubtedly an extreme one, it does show the pressure that one woman felt. The nature of the responsibility which mothers carry is such as to tax the ablest women, for in the last analysis it is the physical and social fitness of several persons that they must promote regardless of the hours or of the energy demanded.

Inability to drop the work in hand because the day seems over-full means less time to interpret the wishes of the children and less apparent concern regarding their interests. To no small degree the younger members of the household, and paid workers when they are members of the household, serve as barometers of the moods of the adults in the family. Frequently the opportunities for privacy in the home are so lacking that the fatigued husband or wife must continue to be a member of the group when the effect of his or her presence upon relationships is harmful. Lack of space for the uninterrupted play or concentration of the members of the group also taxes to the breaking point one's powers of self-control. It is the housing, too, which often accounts for the friction that is caused by a failure to assume responsibilities in the care of one's possessions.

With friction, as with anxiety, the difficulties arise most frequently over the behavior of children. The standard which is held for conduct by one or both parents is very different from the behavior which the child exhibits. With the older children there may be open disagreement on the point at issue. Individual differences seem to necessitate one method with one child and a very different one with another, thus creating what appears to be partiality to the child against whom there has been discrimination. The task of being the family peacemaker makes a heavy demand upon the self-control of the parent and his ability to deal justly with the many appeals for a decision.

In some instances parents do not agree on what is desirable, and in other instances the methods of reaching the goals held in common are debated with more or less open minds. If there are relatives who have a part in handling the younger members, there is likely to be open or suppressed conflict and unhappiness. One person is lax, while another is strict, or both are playing for the central place in the affections of the child.

In contrast with other studies which have been made of family relationships, there is very little evidence of the maladjustment of husband and wife. Since this study was directed largely toward objective problems in connection with management and child development, it may well be that these maladjustments would be shown up only indirectly, if at all. In a few instances the jealousy of husband or wife is indicated; in others the differences in ages and in the degree or type of education seem to create something of a barrier which lessens the amount of satisfaction gained from marriage. The approval and encouragement which are likely to be a part of the reward in business and professional positions outside the home are missed in homemaking by a few, although this lack is not stated as a cause of friction.

Queries for the Student of Family Life.—Those interested in stabilizing family life and in making it more deeply satisfying to the women who no longer consider it the one course open to their sex, see in this study of a small group of highly selected families some of the difficulties for which help is needed. While there is a consensus of opinion that the ultimate rewards are well worth the sacrifices, these women are conscious of the many tests with which they are confronted. Remembering that the group who coöperated in this study are well above the average in ability and in the fund of information which they bring to the conduct of their homes, as well as in the size of their incomes, the question of the nature and the degree of fatigue, worry, and friction in other types of home needs to be raised and data assembled. It is possible that a group in which over seven out of every ten are college graduates of courses in home economics may be over-solicitous in their desire to maintain high standards for their homes and for the behavior of their children, thus occasioning an undue amount of worry and physical labor. On the other hand, the training which they have received should have increased the skill with which they handle the duties of each day and the perspective with which they approach problems that arise. Further, it would seem reasonable to believe that the interest which they evidenced in the study by their willingness to coöperate in it does point to a perspective on management and family life which is very much above the average. What would cross-sections of other types of homes reveal, and to what degree would the findings recorded in the preceding pages be verified or altered?

The length of the working day and the weariness of muscles and nerves point to the need for more information on what constitutes a reasonable load for the mother of young children to carry if she is to maintain a reserve of energy and continue to find zest in the companionship of the family members and in the contacts outside of the home. This lack of information is in striking contrast with the fund of facts regarding a day's work for employees in industry. Even though there is a wide variation in the abilities of the workers and the types of work which they do, employers have found that it is possible to set limits which result in greater efficiency and that it is profitable to maintain a lower rate of productivity over a longer period of time. The twelve-hour day in factories has ceased to be regarded as good business, and the advisability of night work is questioned. A plan which provides for one day of rest in seven is upheld for economic, not religious, reasons. When similar standards are set up for homemaking, supplementary aid from society, if that is necessary, may be more economical in the long run than the use of mother-power to the point where the mother is less fit for widening the horizons and deepening the appreciations of the younger members or for stimulating comradeship with her husband.

It is something of a paradox that a deluge of labor-saving devices, new sources of power, more commercial agencies in the community, and an actual decrease in the size of families have not prevented homemaking from being more than a full-time job. Is the present situation due to the inability of women to evaluate the more and the less important responsibilities? Are homemakers likely to accept without question traditional standards of an earlier generation or of the community in which they live? In other words, is fatigue a *necessary* accompaniment of modern homemaking if the attitude toward family life is constructive, if there is a thoughtful evaluation of the number, frequency, and methods of doing tasks, and if the wife and mother is physically fit? Should we attribute a part of the fatigue to greater dissatisfaction and less willingness to accept the routine of housework which may seem drudgery to many modern women in an age which is more largely pleasure-seeking and leisure-demanding than earlier eras have been? The replies in this study suggest some of the difficulties; they do not clearly define the causes.

Worry and friction have appeared to grow out of fatigue and a lack of knowledge regarding human nature from childhood to adulthood. If fatigue could be measurably reduced and if both husband and wife not only knew the principles underlying the behavior of human beings, but applied them in every-day relationships, would family life be more satisfying because the unattainable would not be expected and the methods of avoiding conflict would be known? Does the fact that this particular group of parents is worrying about the development of children more than about other questions of homemaking point to a need for more emphasis upon the successful methods which parents have used and are using? If there is created in parents insecurity and fear, parental educa-

tion will have performed a service of doubtful value to
family life and child development.

The degree to which it is possible and desirable to
have a home released from worry, fatigue, and friction is
in itself a question. The very fact that the institution is
a developing one in which situations change from year
to year suggests some of the difficulties which would not
be found in a more static unit. While it is probably true
that there is an irreducible minimum for each of these
three factors, the amount in excess of the minimum probably does not serve as an impetus to more successful family life. On the contrary, intelligent control of the activities and relationships within the home can go far toward releasing physical and mental energy for other
purposes.

CHAPTER IV

SOME FACTORS AFFECTING ACHIEVEMENT IN FAMILY LIFE

IN THE PRESENT CHAPTER some of the factors affecting achievement in family life most apparent in the group of families studied are assembled. Chart II focuses attention upon the interrelationships that were brought out by the data when they were analyzed after the manner of case studies rather than being subjected to statistical treatment. The veritable maze of lines appearing portrays "the entangling alliances" that any consideration of the subject involves.

No goal or achievement is the result of a single factor. For example, economic soundness is more than a matter of having an income; the physical constitutions of the members of the group, particularly of the income earners, their vocational fitness, the managerial ability of those who direct the use of the income, and the ability of the others in the group all affect the degree of economic soundness which the family enjoys over a period of years, with the resources of the community constituting an additional factor. Thus there are some households that are always on the verge of bankruptcy quite regardless of the money income; others seem rich in this world's goods although the financial assets are relatively limited. ·

To take another example, that of physical and mental health, one cannot always charge to poor constitutions the items of illness or near illness, important though this factor is. Lack of funds to take the ounces of prevention that help to insure health, the type of physical plant—meaning by this term the dwelling, the grounds, and the equip-

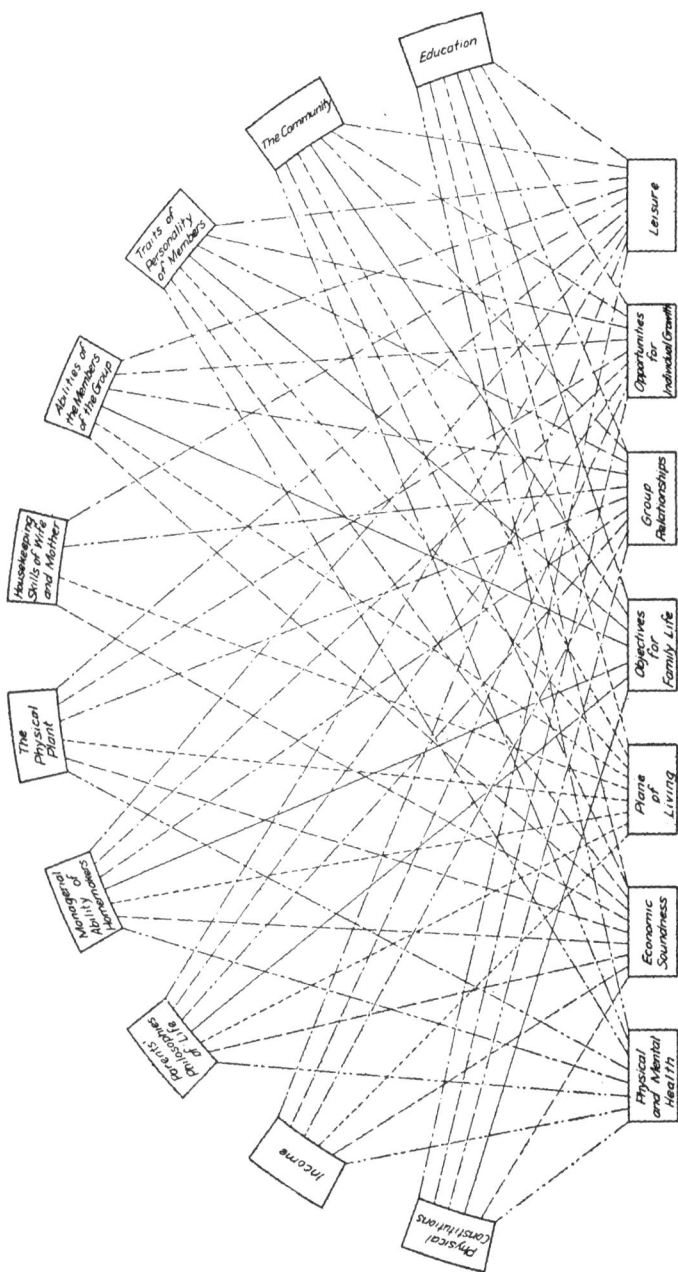

CHART II.—Some Factors Affecting Achievements in Family Life

ment—the managerial ability of the homemakers, and the community in which the family lives are four of the additional influences with which one must reckon before attempting an explanation of the existing state of health.

Just as no one result can be attributed to a single factor, so no factor affects only one objective or achievement. In the following pages the pervasive nature of each of ten factors is discussed and some of the relationships are pointed out.

Physical Constitutions.—If a sound body and a sound mind are the possession of each member of a family the group has an extremely valuable asset. Granted that they receive a reasonable amount of intelligent care, there is a strong likelihood that a continuing high standard of physical and mental health will be enjoyed. This, in turn, makes other conditions for harmonious family life more nearly attainable. The expenditure required for maintaining good health in families where each member has the heritage of organic soundness is relatively low, thus removing from the household account sheet a source of depletion of the income that sometimes knows no upper limits, so great a proportion of the earnings does it demand for doctors, hospitals, dental services, household services, and costly vacations, in addition to the decreased earnings which illness is likely to cause. In other words, economic soundness is less difficult to insure if adults and children are not readily susceptible to disorder and disease of mind or body. Accordingly, the plane of living which can be maintained by the group is determined in part by the organic fitness.

Physical and mental soundness of the family also promotes freedom from fatigue and from anxiety. The degree to which frequent illness decreases the reserve of physical and nervous energy is so commonly observed on every hand that it needs only to be mentioned. Leisure for the pursuit of avocations is more than a matter of free time; it requires enthusiasm and energy as well. Chronic or frequent illnesses of the members of a group make inroads upon the potential uses of the hours away from work. While it is true that these misfortunes may provide a cementing influence for relationships, there is a question whether this effect is more common than the opposite one—that of overtaxing one's willingness to assume additional responsibility and to make allowances over-long for the ailing member.

Income.—The size, the regularity, the certainty, and the sources of the income are considerations of no slight importance in furthering goals. Without desiring to overemphasize the financial factor, it seems fair to say that the dependence of the family of the present generation upon a money income to a degree hitherto unknown makes such considerations as the ones mentioned above more important than they have been in any preceding generation when more of the goods and services were furnished by and in the family group. The question of children's allowances, for example, is likely to be of little moment only to those who are thinking in terms of the few uses which the child of a generation or two ago had for money.

Physical and mental health are more readily purchasable when there is a margin in the income that encourages a family to use money for the ounces of prevention without hazarding its economic security. This has already been pointed out[1] in an indication of the relation which exists between income and health. So, too, the

[1] See p. 54.

duration and bad effects of illness are likely to be lessened if there are adequate funds for care and treatment.

That there is a close relationship between the size and certainty of the income and economic soundness needs no proof, although it may be well to repeat the statement that a large income does not necessarily result in solvency nor is a small income synonymous with insolvency. The rather direct effect that the money income of a family has upon its plane of living is another of the more or less obvious relationships. A family with a small income cannot afford to live for an indefinite length of time in a costly neighborhood nor to become members of a social set that does not have to count the costs of entertainment and of membership in clubs. There may be a liberal expenditure for one or more items in the family budget—those that seem most important to the group—but economies and even sacrifices in other items will then be necessary. After all is said and done a given sum of money will buy *some* of the goods and services which a family desires; it is seldom that *all* of the wants can be supplied even when the income in itself permits a fair degree of comfort.

Although initial objectives for the family life may be, and often are, formulated quite independently of the income, the limitations which it sets upon material goals and the possessions which larger earning power insures are appreciated by those experienced in making both ends meet. The desire to own a home which typifies one's ideal is one thing; the actual ownership of it is quite another. An ambition to bring up a large family becomes for some a vanishing ideal when the costs are estimated. The advisability of taking time to secure an advanced degree, or of living in an environment which offers a maximum of satisfaction to the group, cannot be decided apart from a consideration of the probable future income as well as the present resources. While it is true that there are certain types of objectives which are less directly affected by the income, there is a considerable group of objectives which are closely related to the earnings.

The amount of leisure and the hours when it is available are also controlled in part by the earnings of the family. If the salary is small and the needs are many, there is a tendency for both husband and wife to use the most of their waking hours for services which increase the purchasing power of the income either by adding dollars or by making the dollars go further. For example, a woman may accept a part-time or full-time position in addition to homemaking in order to supplement her husband's salary. In other homes time for diversion and companionship are often crowded out or greatly lessened in order that the mother may get on without paid service for the various activities of the household. Hours for business are likely to have no upper limits in the schedule of the husband that he may insure more of the comforts for the family.

If, on the other hand, there is less need to count the financial costs of time off from housekeeping or business, days are less likely to seem over-full. Fatigue, another of the results found in varying degrees in homes, is measurable in part by the hours of work and the strain which the work brings. Shorter working hours, accompanied by a wise use of leisure, other things being equal, decrease the amount of fatigue; long hours of work and responsibility greatly reduce the reserve in energy.

Just as the matter of family objectives is somewhat dependent upon the income, so the opportunities for individual growth are increased or lessened by the financial status of the family. Fortunately development is not solely a question of money, and the adults with few opportunities in childhood often are proof that money is not essential. Parents, however, who recognize the special abilities in their children may be without the means to develop them. In contrast, one finds the group that has a margin in its income more able to provide the musical, the artistic, or the professional training which helps to insure an individual well equipped to secure for himself and to give to others the satisfactions that arise from the possession of talents or from interest in various fields.

The character of the relationships existing among the members seems to be somewhat associated with the income, although here again there is no basis for inferring that the latter is a sole determinant. As is indicated throughout this chapter, it is but one of the influences which affect the satisfaction and the understanding of each member. For example, the question of where the income comes from and the part that the wife has in supplying it may be a source of friction; the degree of economic freedom which wife or older children have may affect the happiness of the group; and the husband's inability to provide adequately for the needs of the group is, for some, a cause of open or suppressed dissatisfaction. In this connection it may be well to note that the financial status of the family is likely to affect the standing of the group in the community, the associations which the members make, and the demands which the child of high school age makes, thus contributing to the happiness or unhappiness of one or more of the members.

The Parents' Philosophies of Life.—There was a variation

in the degree of happiness and satisfaction in the families studied which pointed to factors other than good constitutions and an adequate income as in part responsible for attitudes and relationships. After having read and reread the statements, having compared and contrasted the replies to the questions asked, and having attempted to summarize the reasons for the variations found, it does not seem an overstatement of the case to suggest that the outlook on life which both parents have affects to a considerable degree the atmosphere of the home and the nature of associations which exist between the members.

The bearing of one's philosophy upon relationships is particularly evident in one home where the wife's interest in accuracy and perfection for each member of the household had done away with any possibility of relaxation or refreshment for the husband and children. They were less interested than the mother in making of life a routine in which each became a slave to meticulousness. In this family the husband's attitude was one of interest in system only as a means to an end, and that end was the more harmonious associations of those within and without the home. The vast difference in the philosophy of husband and wife was at least one factor which kept the home from providing the members of the group with the satisfactions which each wanted. In addition to the havoc that this difference wrought in group relationships and in the opportunities for individual growth, there were evidences of an excessive amount of fatigue, accompanied by considerable anxiety, and leisure in a miserly amount, with few of the returns which even a small portion might be expected to bring.

In striking contrast with the situation in the family described above was the home in which the mother refused to believe that life was made up entirely of problems, although the number recorded for her to solve and the difficulties which they would suggest to many persons exceeded those found in the former home. Chronic illness of the husband, with all of the adjustments which his illness involved, did not seem to overwhelm her. On the contrary, she stated that the years brought opportunities and challenges, instead of problems, and that it was her desire to see how satisfactorily she could meet each one. The attitude of her husband indicated agreement and cooperation. Together they appeared to have gone a long way in laying a foundation for their home life which resulted in a large measure of satisfaction and growth for all of the members.

With the data at hand it has not seemed possible to analyze the influences which have been responsible for building up the existing philosophies of these parents; yet it is exceedingly important to know—if there is a satisfactory method of finding the reasons—why some people seem always to view life through darkly colored glasses while others accept it enthusiastically and allow no obstacle, no matter how difficult, to keep them out of sight of their objectives. Certainly no question has a more significant bearing upon family life and child development. The further ramifications of the philosophy of the parents in the home are shown in Chart II.

The Managerial Ability of the Homemakers.—As has been pointed out in an earlier connection the size of the income in itself does not guarantee economic soundness nor cause economic dependence. Neither does it prescribe the plane of living any more than it does of itself insure health, leisure, good group relationships, individual growth, or material objectives for family life. To be sure, however, many of these may be more nearly within reach theoretically, if the financial resources are beyond the mere subsistence level.

It is not what one has but what one does with what one has that determines the outcome. And so it seems to be with physical constitutions, with income, with other possessions of economic value in the home and in the community, and with the human assets of the family. It is the degree to which the heads of families are able to plan, direct, and control the resources, both human and material, that helps to determine how efficient will be their use and how satisfactory will be the resulting atmosphere for each of the members. In other words, physical and mental health, economic soundness, objectives for family life, a desired plane of living, leisure, opportunities for growth, and harmonious group relationships are more likely to result in homes where there is more than average managerial ability. If this ability is confined to one or the other of the parents in the enterprise of homemaking, instead of being present in both, the task of insuring the conditions previously listed will be more difficult to perform with an equal measure of success, particularly if there is a lack of appreciation, of coöperation, or of concern on the part of the one with less managerial ability. *The Physical Plant.*—The importance which the majority of women and many of the men who coöperated in this study attached to the physical plant—a term which is used here to include the dwelling, grounds, furnishings, and equipment—appears to be justified when one studies the relation that it bears to health, economic soundness, the plane of living, the objectives for family life, the amount and uses of leisure, the opportunities for growth, and group relationships. Without going into too great detail in regard to the contribution that a physical plant makes to each of these conditions, it has seemed wise to illustrate certain connections. A dwelling which is either too large or too small, one which is poorly arranged or without modern conveniences, one which lacks suitable indoor and outdoor space for children and grown-ups, or one which lacks the furnishings and equipment that promote convenience, comfort, and group living makes achievement much more difficult. Indeed, in some cases it seems well-nigh impossible under existing conditions.

Housekeeping Skills of the Wife and Mother.—The degree of expertness with which the wife and mother does the many diverse tasks connected with housekeeping and homemaking is a matter which varies in importance inversely with the size of income and directly with the demands upon it. That is to say, a small income demands a greater degree of ability on the part of the woman if economic soundness is to be maintained and if the members of the group are to be kept happy than does a large one. Waste of material assets through faulty preparation of food is but one of the costs which one can attribute to a lack of skill; a shorter period of usefulness for clothing, linens, or other furnishings due to improper laundering or lack of care is another economic loss. Dissatisfaction and a lack of harmony frequently result if these wastes continue indefinitely and if the other members of the family are sensitive to the imperfections of the meals or of the wardrobes.

The effect of a lack of skill is less noticeable and less tragic if the margin in the income is greater and if skilled services may be hired. For example, when one can afford to use a good laundress who is easily accessible, or when cooked food can be purchased at a price that is not prohibitive, the need for the wife and mother to launder or to cook well is less urgent. Where the opportunities for securing skilled service are few, the need for training the unskilled helpers makes at least a fair degree of skill on the part of the wife and mother desirable if wastes are to be prevented and satisfactory standards are to be maintained.

Abilities of the Members of the Household.—In addition to the managerial ability of the parents and the skills involved in homemaking which seem relatively important for the wife and mother, the abilities of the other members in the household and the degree of competency of both husband and wife in various fields of endeavor have their effects upon the home. The ages of the children and the attention which has been paid to the formation of habits in the early years help to determine how independent each one is in caring for his own wants. They determine, too, how useful each one is in assisting with the routine tasks of the household, thus affecting the amount of leisure for the adults in the group and the opportunities for recreation as a group. The degree to which the children and the father share regularly in the daily and seasonal activities also affects the plane of living and the economic soundness of the home. Other things being equal, the more able and willing the members are to assume responsibility the less is the drain made upon the mother's strength or upon the family's purse for paid service.

The effect of skilled paid workers has already been mentioned. Obviously the more varied the ability of the helper, the greater the release of the wife and mother from routine duties, provided she is willing to relinquish an increased share of the routine. If, on the contrary, she thinks that she cannot trust the preparation of food or the laundering or the care of the children to another, this means of procuring leisure is less effective for her. Occasionally, too, this very unwillingness to give the worker increased responsibility may prove a handicap in the relation with the employee, and more frequent turnover may result.

Abilities of the several members of a family in school achievement, in occupations, in avocations, or in other fields contribute to the interests, the atmosphere, and the objectives for the individual and the group. For example, a woman who has had a successful and deeply satisfying career before marriage may discover that she and the other members of the family are happier when she continues with these outside interests. The result may be an income in money double that which the husband alone could earn, thus encouraging a very different plane of living or greater economic security in the form of investments. In another home the policy of combining homemaking with another career may be so objectionable to the husband, relatives, or children that it becomes a source of serious family friction.

Musical talent, ability in sketching, an interest in dramatics or in writing, when possessed by one or more members and recognized by others in the group, is likely to affect the items of the budget, the expenditure of time, the opportunities provided, and the goals formulated. A wide variation in abilities within the group may help to account for—if it does not entirely explain—the jealousies and the inferiority complexes which are sometimes found in families.

Personality Traits of the Members of the Household.— Personality traits may be either assets or liabilities on the family balance sheet. Regardless of the side of the ledger on which they are set down, they need to be reckoned with as a factor affecting achievement. In the case of the very young child the effect is less apparent, for his personality is in the making and he has a much smaller part in the affairs of the household. Defects are less likely to upset the group of which he is a member than faults in the parents who are in the position of directors. With increasing age and responsibility self-control or a violent temper, selfishness or unselfishness, willingness to reason rather than rationalize, jealousy or a lack of it, thrift or extravagance, thoughtfulness or lack of consideration, and supersensitiveness as opposed to greater objectivity are but a few of the traits that one finds. These and others influence the degree of economic soundness, the accepted plane of living, the quality of group relationships, the opportunities for individual growth, the use of leisure, and the objectives for family life.

The Community.—The days when a man's home was his castle are gone. On every hand there are evidences of the degree to which the modern family must depend upon and is, in fact, at the mercy of the community in which it lives. Nor does the relationship end here. With widened markets and the inter-play of economic forces in different, but no longer independent, regions, the wealth and welfare of the family are in part the effect of national policies and practices. A more detailed discussion of what this dependence means to the modern family is found in Chapter VIII. In the present connection only a few examples of the relationship are presented.

The germ theory of disease has long ago made people realize that public sanitation and the prevention of disease by isolation, vaccination, and legislation are essential if individuals are to be protected from epidemics and from frequent illness. The attention given to education in character-building and to the prevention of delinquency points to a growing realization on the part of communities that a high standard of social fitness is partly a matter of environment and that the blame for all deviations from the normal and desirable cannot justly be laid wholly upon heredity. So, too, economic soundness and the plane of living are not merely the results of good management on the part of two individuals. They are dependent in a large measure upon the facilities that the community provides for earning and using.

It is not possible to say how largely the associations and the institutions of the community affect the degree and the character of the relationships between the members of the family. That the extra-curricular activities of schools greatly lessen the time that many adolescent children have at home is a frequent comment from the parents. They feel, too, that the standards of expenditure set for the teen age girl or boy often promote difficulties in the home. In addition there are the problems that grow out of a difference in their objectives for family life and those which other families set for themselves. These, in turn, affect the opportunities for individual growth and for the employment of leisure.

Emphasis has frequently been placed upon the fact that the individual members make up the community and that their desires can be realized by group action. If however, those who covet other standards for their families are in the minority, or if there is indifference on the part of a considerable number, the changes will be impossible of accomplishment.

Education.—Education may be regarded as a part of the

environment, and in that event it is logically included under the community. But because it is related not alone to the existing conditions, it seems preferable to consider it separately that it may receive a larger emphasis.

The parents have their present philosophies of life, their degree of vocational fitness, their several abilities, including that of management, and their traits of personality as a result, in part at least, of the education, both formal and informal, which they have received at home, in school, and in the other earlier associations of life. In this heritage one finds a partial explanation of the status which they have, the goals which they seek, the relationships which they display, and the tests which they use in making evaluations. While it is true that the present opportunities and needs are influencing their beliefs and customs, there is a question of the extent of that influence in comparison with the earlier training. Study classes are of importance in directing attention to the methods used in teaching children, and books and magazines are helpful in encouraging thought and knowledge along particular lines. The saying that one is never too old to learn holds true, but the previous influences are not readily overbalanced by the newer learning.

It is for precisely this reason that the educational opportunities provided for the younger generation seem important to the parents. There is a consciousness that what the child gets early affects his lifelong habits and attitudes; and that the traits, the skills, and the knowledge acquired during the years of rapid development make a contribution not alone to his childhood home, but that these are indispensable in fitting him for later life. Thus the type and the amount of education help to bring about certain conditions of thought and action which affect two generations of families very directly.

Summary.—In the preceding pages there has been an attempt to list the factors in a selected group of families which seemed most frequently related to certain objectives and achievements of family life. The importance of the physical constitution, of the income, the parents' philosophies of life, the managerial ability of the homemakers, the physical plant, the housekeeping skills of the wife and mother, other abilities and traits of the individual members, the community, and education is brought out again and again. It is entirely possible that there are other factors which have not come out in this study, designed, as it was, to secure information on attitudes and practices of management and child development, and that some of these are as important as those mentioned, perhaps even more important. They were not, however, sufficiently clear from the data available to justify their inclusion in this list.

The pervasive nature of each of the factors observed makes the matter of securing desired ends in family life far less simple than that resulting from the application of a single formula. Good group relationships result from more than a desire to get on well with others, and leisure is not available merely because the physical plant is convenient, though this is one of the important factors. An appreciation of these interrelationships is essential for those who would do constructive work in helping to build family life in the present era.

CHAPTER V

SOME ECONOMIC NEEDS OF FAMILIES

THE IMPORTANCE that this selected group of men and women attach to material prosperity is perhaps not greater than that to be found among other types of families, although it is probable that their educational advantages may have made certain desires seem more important than those same desires would be to others who have had a very different background of experience and training. On the other hand, there are evidences that traits of personality, together with educational opportunities, have resulted in a perspective which gives to economic status only a proportionate share of attention in formulating goals for the group. The less tangible values in life seem to many more to be desired than large money incomes.

The fact that a large percentage of the men who are earning have not yet reached the zenith of their power and that many of the homes have been established recently needs to be remembered in reviewing the comments of the group. Large expenditures required for establishing a home, and in many cases a business enterprise in addition, heavy demands made upon the current income by the coming of children, and the costs of securing further professional training are frequent in such a group. In the present chapter the conditions which increase the pressure upon the financial resources of the family and the problems which these conditions create are presented.

Sources and Adequacy of the Income.—An adequate income earned under conditions which do not interfere with successful family life is a recognized need. One of the reasons which is frequently given by wives and mothers for accepting part-time or full-time employment is the necessity of increasing the income in order that a satisfactory plane of living may be maintained. Whether this is truly the *basic* reason in the majority of cases, or whether other reasons growing out of earlier economic freedom, professional recognition, and routine of a type which is different from that of homemaking, offer the explanation, cannot be satisfactorily determined. Undoubtedly, however, the desire for an increasing number and quantity of the goods and services which money will buy is encouraged by educational advantages. Conveniences, comforts, attractive surroundings, and opportunities for growth become a part of the necessities rather than of the luxuries of life. Once an appreciation of literature, music, and the other fine arts has been gained, it is much harder to formulate a standard or to live upon a plane which does not include the means of enjoying them, either through individual possession or patronage of agencies for their support.

When the advantages regarded as important for the well-being of the family require more than the husband can provide from his earnings, the methods of supplying the additional funds involve many adjustments. Certainly some of them are costly when viewed in terms of the ultimate effect upon the individual and the group. This seems to be the case where the employment of mothers outside the home, or their absorption in a remunerative occupation within the home, results in a less competent type of care and supervision for the children. It is also true in cases where the expenditure of energy by women who are engaged in two occupations, either for part or full time, is so great that there is no reserve left for group comradeship and the associations of family life. In other words, when the demands of an occupation and the management of the home, even though the actual routine of providing physical care for the family is delegated to others, leave little strength, time or desire for leisure with husband and children, the advantages *for the family* from an increased money income are likely to be outweighed by the disadvantages. That the opposite of this effect does obtain in some instances appears to be true. In such instances, the second occupation serves as a means of promoting more satisfactory relationships in addition to increasing the financial assets of the family. This effect is noted particularly when the occupation is one for which the woman has had special training and one which brings her satisfaction, and when both husband and children are entirely in accord with her desire to combine earning with homemaking.

One of the methods by which the income is supplemented without having the wife leave home is that of taking roomers or boarders. While this method has an advantage in that it permits mothers to continue the care and supervision of their children, the presence of other persons in the household, unless the dwelling is planned for this need, may interfere more or less seriously with the degree of privacy which can be secured by parents and children. If those outside the family have their meals in the home, the energy, the time, and the patience of the mother may be taxed quite as much as if she were carrying a full-time position outside the home. In addition, the opportunity for outside interests may be greatly limited as a result of the confining nature of preparing three meals daily when there is little or no paid service.

Another method of supplementing the income which

was reported by several in the group studied was that of substitute teaching. From the point of view of the need for a definite and periodic addition to one husband's earnings this seemed highly unsatisfactory. Quite as unsatisfactory did this method appear in the conduct of the household. Calls to act as a supply teacher in cases of illness or of other emergencies permit little planning in advance, and, as a result, the family may be less satisfactorily cared for during the time when the wife is away. Furthermore, the irregularity of such employment makes the need for paid service one for which many families hesitate to provide. The increased cost of meals away from home and of occasional service, which is always more expensive, may very nearly deplete the added earnings. The variety of the demands which are made upon a substitute teacher and the difficulties of adjustment create a strain which makes this method of supplementing the earnings a less desirable one for the welfare of the group.

Because 85 per cent of the children in the families studied were under ten years of age, reference to children's earnings, which is found to such a large extent in studies of families of wage-earners, was not made. Even in the case of the older children they were not regarded as potential contributors to the money income by their parents, whose goal for sons and daughters was a physical and educational foundation which would enable earning on a higher level in adulthood. There was no evidence of this group's being penny-wise and pound-foolish in their effort to enlarge the family income by the services of younger members.

As has been intimated, it is not alone the size of the income that is of importance, but the conditions under which it is secured, that need to be considered. That the process of earning by the father should not prevent him from being a companion and a teacher in the family has probably less frequently been regarded as a condition necessary for the promotion of successful family life. This attitude is due in part to the fact that the woman is considered by many to be *the* homemaker in the group and that the husband's share is contributed when he has provided the funds necessary for the needs.

Throughout this study there are evidences of the direct effect which long hours, the heavy pressure of competition, and demands allied to earning have upon the husband and father, and of the indirect effect which they produce upon the group as a whole. When the mother must serve as the sole counselor because the father has little time at home when the children are awake, or because he is "too tired to be bothered," the child is deprived of an association on which he has a claim. Furthermore, when excessive demands connected with earning a livelihood are made upon the husband, excessive demands are likely to be made upon the mother in the guidance of and companionship with the younger members. The division of labor is too complete a one to provide the advantages which come from a sharing of experiences and a fusion of interests.

In brief, an income should not only be adequate, but it should be earned under conditions which do not deplete the energy or the hours necessary for the welfare of the group. Fatigue and anxiety are foes of fitness that greatly diminish the possibility of family life. They are no less destructive in their effects when they occur among fathers than when they exist among mothers.

There is no attempt here to set up figures that represent an adequate income for the professional man and his family. The needs of one group are likely to vary from that of another. A number of factors may make a salary which seems ample for one family too small to insure economic security in another household. The number in the family, the ages of the members, their states of health, the cost of living in the community, the professional obligations, particularly of the husband, and the abilities of the individuals in the group all affect the amount that is required. The most that can be said is that in families where the total sum received is too small to maintain a plane of living which is comparable with the standard the group is attempting to reach, supplementary sources of varying degrees of desirability are tapped. When these sources include the earnings of mothers, the results for family well-being are likely to be satisfactory only if the community in which the group lives insures substitutes for a part of the homemaking services at a price that can be afforded by the family. Finally, if the employment of either fathers or mothers lessens their success as companions and teachers, the financial gains are in time outweighed by the sacrifices which result.

Certainty and Regularity of the Money Income.—Certainty and regularity of the money income decrease the frequency and the intensity of financial and related problems. A lack of information regarding the probable annual earnings keeps many families from adopting principles of business management. Proportionate using is possible only when one knows both the needs and the total sum available over a given period. Without this information about the income, a decision regarding the wisdom of adding a new coat to the wardrobe, of making another investment, or of having an operation for a chronic ailment cannot be made intelligently. As a result the conservative and thrifty manager is likely to err on the side of an indefinite postponement, while the optimistic one secures the goods or services hoping that both ends will meet when the time of reckoning arrives. In some cases summaries of previous assets serve as a very satisfactory guide to what one can expect, but in other cases the wide fluctuation in amount makes any estimates at most a guess. This is particularly true when the occupation is farming,[1] in which one has no control over the weather and relatively slight control over market conditions. This is also true when the income is made up largely of commissions or fees. The position of the family on a definite salary, even though a small one, is a position to be envied from the viewpoint of ease in planning for the needs of the group.

A lack of regularity in the dates when the income can be expected is another handicap in the use of the earnings in any systematic fashion. To buy white goods in the January sales or the winter's supply of vegetables in the fall may be recognized as good management by the household buyer, but, if she has no margin for purchasing such supplies at the time when prices are low, economy be-

[1] Quoting from King, *The National Income and Its Purchasing Power*, the dilemma of the farmer and his family is made evident: "When all quantities are expressed in dollars of constant purchasing power, the income of all farmers was roughly stationary between 1909 and 1915, then rose sharply until 1918, declined somewhat in 1919, fell off rapidly in 1920, and tumbled precipitously in 1921. The much heralded prosperity of the farmer in 1918 and his poverty in 1921, were then, no mere figments of the imagination, for the total income of all farmers in 1921 would buy but slightly more than half as many direct goods as would their income in 1918. The purchasing power of the income of all farmers taken as a unit increased regularly each year from 1921 until 1927 with a slight decline in 1926. By 1923 it was approximately the figure for 1915 which was considered a good year for agriculture. The income in 1925 was about half way between the income of 1915 and that of 1916, in both of which years the farmers were sharing in the prosperity brought on by European war orders."—P. 307.

comes of necessity a secondary consideration. For the family with a small accumulation of capital and a limit upon the amount of credit which it can secure, a knowledge that the first of the month or the beginning of the quarter will mean a definite fund for the uses of the family reduces the degree of anxiety felt by those who are responsible for the policies of the group. In the matter of children's allowances as in other allotments, one can work the plan more successfully when the total amount is known.

Another problem that arises out of irregularity is in the nature of a temptation to use the assets unwisely. This is seen particularly when there are red letter days, on which a large share of the annual income is received, interspersed among months during which there is little or no ready money. An example is noted in the after-harvest period for the rural family, provided there is a margin after the expenses of the crop and the interest on mortgages are paid.

The family whose income is both uncertain and irregular in whole or large part, as is the case with the family of the farmer, of many professional men, and of the owner of a business is at a double disadvantage in planned spending. As the capital which has been accumulated is increased and the investments are spread over a greater number of securities, the diversified earnings from season to season make the risks less and the margin greater, thereby reducing the difficulties which arise from fluctuating and unstable returns on labor and capital. In other words, the family whose total assets never provide more than a narrow margin above that required for physical needs is in a more precarious position as a result of an uncertain and irregular income than is the one which has a sufficiently large return, irregular though it may be, to tide them over a business depression or a heavy drain on the earnings.

The effect of an uncertain apportionment for household expenditures, despite the fact that the total income may be known, is also evident among the families studied.

Regardless of the amount of knowledge which the husband may have concerning the family's financial condition, a failure or an unwillingness to acquaint his wife and older children—in fact all members of the group who have a share in using it—with the condition makes intelligent use much less probable and the causes of dissatisfaction more numerous. The difficulties which are created for the wife who assumes a major share in directing the financial affairs upon the death of her husband are also seen. Wholly unversed in business transactions and the events which have preceded present conditions, she finds herself at the mercy of paid advisers who are often less interested in her welfare than they are in their own prosperity.

Effect of Changed Standards of Living.—Changed standards of living of present-day families alter the nature and the extent of the demands upon incomes. The concept of what constitutes an adequate income is a changing one. A comparison of the goods and services which were regarded as essential by a middle class family of a generation ago with those that the laborer has today indicates the rising plane of living. A comparison of the prices of retail commodities reveals the changes in the cost of living. These differences affect the nature and the extent of the demands which are made upon money incomes.

One of the respects in which the standard of living in the United States has shown the greatest advance since the turn of the century has been in the matter of housing. Although running water, furnaces, and electricity were the exception in many sections of the country but a few decades ago, today they are regarded as necessities by the families of professional men, and by many other groups whose standards in other respects are vastly different; there is an increasing appreciation of the comforts and conveniences which good housing can bring, and there is much greater dissatisfaction with the type which was considered luxurious even by the parents of the present generation. Space that was regarded not long ago as ample for sleeping is "crowding" for many groups today. Psychologists are seeking to encourage still greater privacy than that now provided, on the ground that too little privacy for the individual is likely to affect permanently his emotional development.

The greatly increased mobility of the population and the exceedingly high land values that have accompanied the rise of the modern industrial order have added to the housing problem. In a day of big business and almost daily mergers of corporations a man's work is shifted from one city to another, often making the ownership of a home a white elephant. In addition, there are the limitations which ordinances and statutes put upon the individual's freedom to hire a contractor and to "put up" a house, as formerly, on a lot which he owns. The type of structure which will be permitted, the conditions which must be met in the use of materials and construction— even to the minimum cost which will be allowed in many instances—and the various improvements which must be provided are prescribed in building codes. Pavements, water, sewerage systems, and other improvements require expenditures which increase the cost of ownership.

As a result of this combination of circumstances many families on moderate incomes question the advisability of *tying up several thousand dollars in homes of their own. They are conscious, too, of the variations in the demands which a growing family makes, a fact which only serves to increase the disadvantage of a dwelling which may be very satisfactory at one stage of development. In other words, a large proportion of their savings, both present and future, is required to provide for a need which changes considerably with changes in the ages of the members, the nature and the location of the man's occupation, and the improvements in housing. The alternative of paying rent to a landlord frequently seems the lesser of two evils, particularly if the location is a temporary one and the pressure upon the income is great. Figures regarding the extent of ownership among the 306 families in the present study are lacking, but there are frequent references to the desire for ownership and the apparent inability to finance the type of dwelling which is desired.

The present requisites in housing are less definitely established than are the dietary needs of families, but certain qualities are regarded as extremely desirable. In this item of the budget, as in others, the standard accepted by the professional group is higher than that of other groups. Their requirements include provision for health and safety, privacy, conveniences, comfort, recreational space, opportunities for social life, attractiveness, and a community which promotes the physical, intellectual, and social development of the several members. Testing a given dwelling by these requirements, one can readily understand why the conveniences offered by most city apartments, even if children are permitted, are offset by other lacks and why parents prefer to move into houses for one or two families. Whether this preference will continue to exist depends largely upon the attitude of the property owner, his ability to develop plans which are satisfactory, the provision which he succeeds in making for outdoor space, and the rentals that he charges. One may well raise the question of whether apartments are unsuited to the needs of families living in the present generation or whether the apparent unsuitability is the result of real estate developments by those who, in their eagerness to secure maximum profits from their investments, have been unmindful of the needs of families.

The recognition that the promotion of health is less costly in energy and money than the cure of illness has followed the increased reliance upon a pecuniary order. Absences of the breadwinner from work are doubly costly in that they require not alone the payment of physicians' fees and the accompanying items, but for many the loss of wage or salary during the illness.

Nor are the charges for illness comparable with those incurred in the days of general practitioners who were more or less able to treat all manner of disease. The degree of specialization which exists in the medical profession, the extent to which hospitals, instead of homes, are used to care for illness and convalescence, the increased use of surgery, and the cost of nursing all complicate the problem of affording even the occasional siege of illness. The remark has been made that only the rich are in a position to be ill.

To use but one example, many of the present generation of adults were born in the homes of their parents with only a general practitioner and a neighbor or a relative to provide assistance; today, particularly in urban regions, the children of these same persons are brought into the world after several months during which there have been periodic examinations and advice for the expectant mother. Delivery occurs in a hospital, and this is followed by a two weeks' stay for mother and child, while additional services are paid for in the home. Nor is this all! During the period of infancy the services of an infant specialist—not the obstetrician—are required to give the child a good start. Often, for good measure, as it were, there are additional services for the mother by a dentist. If the wife is employed outside the home, one must add to the costs of having a child the decrease in her earnings. Estimating the cost to the family of a child for the first two years of his life makes one the more appreciative of the reason why families are becoming smaller under modern economic conditions.

The degree to which health is dependent upon proper diet is more clearly perceived as results of research are made available. Pellagra, rickets, malnutrition, and constipation are but a few of the conditions that are directly traceable to faulty diets. The plan of using spring tonics, which used to be a common remedy, has been replaced by the practice of including more milk, eggs, fresh fruits and green vegetables in the menus the year round. But here again new findings regarding the promotion of health increase the costs to the family. The articles of food which prevent disease are more expensive than the starchy foods which, though they yield energy, cannot be relied upon exclusively.

In the era when a larger proportion of the population lived on farms and when production was primarily for use, the recognition of these needs would have caused less difficulty in providing for them, particularly in the growing season. With the present system of indirect distribution and the perishable nature of these needed groups of foods, the cost to the urban consumer is bound to be high. For many the conditions under which they live make even vegetable gardens prohibitive. If one leaves entirely out of consideration the changed standards for food which have resulted from the custom of more elaborate or costly entertaining, and thinks only in terms of the promotion of health, an increase in the per capita allotment for raw materials is still necessary in the budget of many families. Food is one of the items in the budget in which apparent economies may be exceedingly costly.

Another reason why food requires a greater expenditure in the budget of the present-day family is that of the change in the household routine. Churning, canning, bread-making, and to a lesser extent the preparation of other baked foods, have been taken over by outside agencies. More than fifty per cent of this group buy their bread regularly. While this shift of duties from the shoulders of women has reduced the arduousness of their day, it has increased the money cost of food for the family.

Changes in the organization of the household are making other demands upon inelastic incomes, thus decreasing the margin after provision has been made for physical needs. To a very much greater degree than formerly ready-to-wear departments are supplying women and children with their wearing apparel. Ten per cent of the entire group report that they do no sewing at home.

Service for laundering in the home and the use of outside agencies make an additional demand upon the income. The process of dry cleaning is also one which is paid for in money rather than in time and strength of members of the family. Full-time or part-time help with the various household tasks is employed by 50 per cent at prices that are higher in wages, in the cost of food eaten, and in the more extravagant use of materials than was true in earlier generations.

A long life, as pointed out in a previous chapter, does not mean necessarily a prolonged period of earning, though the years of *needing* a money income are lengthened. The custom of retiring from active service, whether because of physical disabilities or at the request of those who are responsible for providing employment, requires that one take thought for the morrow when man lives but works no more. If retirement from the various occupations were accompanied by the granting of annuities to the discharged employees, a lack of foresight and safety in making investments during the years of earning would be less tragic, but the rate of turnover in industry and business, due in part to the desire to better one's condition, makes this a policy upon which but few can count. For those who have a business or a profession of their own, there is only the margin above the needs of business and of their families to provide for the after-earning years.

The large families of a generation ago made possible a relay arrangement in living for parents who were no longer able to work, and this decreased the cost of maintenance considerably for the parents. At the same time the plan of living with one's children was likely to insure a greater degree of oversight of health and comfort. In the present era the decrease in the size of families, smaller dwellings, and a certain pleasure-seeking philosophy of life on the part of those who are still active make the situation brought about with aged parents in the home one which is less likely to be satisfactory for the three generations. The increase in independence that members of both sexes have enjoyed in more recent years is another factor which bids fair to complicate such a situation.

There is another respect in which the less active years may prove to be difficult ones. The investments made during the earning period are frequently of a more haz-ardous nature than formerly when considered in terms of their usefulness during old age; yet dependence upon regular and certain earnings is greater in an era when practically all goods and services must be purchased. For example, frequent changes in location may mean that the owned home with all of its associations, which could be occupied indefinitely if there were money for the taxes, is not one of the assets. As has been pointed out, the cost of an increasing number of goods and services has changed one's idea of the amount that is necessary for a plane to which one has become accustomed. In brief, economic security has become more difficult, more un-certain, and more costly; yet it must be provided over a longer period of time.

The weighing of present advantages for the family against future old age and the proportioning of earnings wisely between the two sets of needs become more of a problem when many of the present advantages seem in-dispensable for success. This conflict in desires is ob-served to a marked degree in the group of families studied, for one finds here the effect of educational op-portunities of the parents upon the standards for the children. In a very large number of their goals, college educations for the children are listed; training in music and an opportunity to attend concerts seem essential; travel is regarded as desirable; shows and the theatre in moderation are not denied a place; and books and magazines cannot be dispensed with, particularly in the more rural areas where libraries are not available.

The needs of the church and of the community have increased along with those of the family, and there is a desire on the part of many of these families to fulfill their responsibilities as church attendants and as citizens. The multiplicity of organizations and of obligations, many of them assumed in college, make the item of membership dues and assessments one which cannot be avoided. Occasional vacations for the family and some entertaining have values which make both desirable. The family car and the radio make additional demands upon the income. And so the list lengthens almost indefinitely! For some the effect of what the neighbors do is not allowed to interfere with what can be afforded; in others there is the sentiment expressed that one cannot be so different as to seem "queer."

Here again decreased isolation makes the standards of other families more important, while the opportunities for "spending money" on every side increase the amount of self-control that is required on the part of both parents and children. The conditions accompanying city life, the dominance of the profit motive in industry, the desire for conspicuous, or at least comparable, display, and the remoteness of the future make intelligent choices in terms of ultimate objectives the more difficult.

Conclusions.—An increased dependence upon money income, unpredictable fluctuations in its regularity, and a lack of certainty regarding the assets upon which the family can count alter the nature and increase the frequency of economic problems which managers of present-day homes encounter. More costly standards of living, the weaknesses in bargaining power that result from lack of organization among consumers, and the dominance of the profit motive in business make the practice of thrift more difficult. These conditions create a need for consumers to have more knowledge regarding the economic order and greater intelligence in the use of material resources. The husbanding of assets cannot be regarded as a matter of importance only for those on the lowest economic levels. Often those with larger incomes find that the more numerous and costly demands in a rising standard of living create a perpetual problem in choice-making and one which taxes to the limit their powers of judgment and of self-control.

CHAPTER VI

SOME EDUCATIONAL NEEDS FOR MARRIAGE AND PARENTHOOD

APART FROM ECONOMIC NEEDS which hamper the attainment of family objectives, and yet related to them, are the educational needs which are disclosed in the attitudes of the men and women coöperating in the present study. To what degree these needs may be those of a cross-section of the population can be determined only when more data are available. For the builder of curricula designed for present and prospective homemakers, however, the findings do suggest some of the points for emphasis and some evaluation of the courses which have been offered in the past. Inasmuch as slightly less than eight out of every ten of the women in the group were college graduates with a major in home economics, there is information on the degree to which the training more closely related to homemaking has been useful for this purpose. Unfortunately the questionnaire which was used did not contain any questions which would throw light on the type of education or the courses that were most useful in preparing the men for their responsibilities in family life.

A checking list of subjects was provided in the questionnaire, and each woman was asked to check those on which she desired more information. The results are recorded in the order of their frequency in Table VII for the group as a whole and for the three sub-groups classified according to the type and amount of formal education each had had. Child training ranks first of all among the recognized needs and is listed by more than seven out of ten for the group as a whole, for the group

TABLE VII

NATURE OF ADDITIONAL TRAINING DESIRED BY WOMEN

Name of Subject	Group A Those without College Degree (53)		Group B Those with Major other than Home Economics (25)		Group C Undergraduate or Graduate Degrees in Home Econ. (228)		All Groups (306)	
	No.	Per Cent	No.	Per Cent	No.	Per Cent	No.	Per Cent
Child Training.........	39	73.1	17	68	179	82.8	235	77.0
Psychology............	30	56.4	14	56	118	51.7	162	52.9
Management..........	27	50.0	10	40	77	33.7	114	37.2
Nutrition.............	20	37.8	5	20	72	31.6	97	31.3
Philosophy and Literature...........	15	28.2	5	20	57	24.5	77	25.1
Household Skills........	13	24.2	10	40	54	23.3	77	25.1
Economics............	17	31.9	6	24	42	18.4	65	21.0
Art.................	9	16.7	6	24	48	21.1	63	20.5
Sociology.............	13	24.2	5	20	37	15.7	55	18.0
Education.............	16	30.0	3	20	27	11.6	46	15.0
Home Nursing, Hygiene, Medicine ...	2	3.6	2	8	5	2.2	9	3.0
Religion..............	..	....	1	4	3	1.2	4	1.2

without college degrees, and for the one in which the major is home economics. More than half of each group believe that they needed a better knowledge of psychology, though a considerable number have had courses in this field.

More than a third of the entire number checked more information on management. This need was recognized by four out of ten in the group of college women with a major other than home economics and by half of those who had not had college degrees. Approximately three in ten consider that more information on nutrition would be helpful. This need, like that of management, was more frequently recognized by the group without college degrees.[1]

For the group as a whole philosophy and literature tie with household skills for fifth place. One in four wants more information on each, but two out of five of those with a major other than home economics have felt the need of more help in household skills. Economics, art, sociology, and education follow in the order named with no one listed by more than three out of ten in any sub-group. In the spaces left to note additional needs there were few suggestions. Home nursing, hygiene, preventive medicine, and religion were mentioned by a few.

The degree of help which college training provided for homemaking was differently regarded within the group who had four years or more in an institution of higher learning. In some instances the replies were qualified in such a way that it was hard to classify them; in other cases the question was not answered. Very nearly one half of all the graduates believed that the training could have been more helpful, while less than one in ten replied with an unconditional no. In this connection it is interesting to note that but one in three of the graduates with a major other than home economics thought college courses could have been more helpful for homemaking, whereas the ratio for the latter group was approximately one in every two. Whether this comparison points to the recognition of a closer relation between the curriculum and the home in the case of the women who have had home economics training is not clear. The size of the non-home-economics group may be a factor making for the contrast in point of view. One in three

[1] As will be seen in Table I there were only 53 in this group. Resulting percentages should be viewed in the light of this fact.

indicates that experience in the home is essential for an appreciation of the nature of the responsibilities which homemaking involves. Regardless of the factors that entered into the group opinions there is an expression on the part of a considerable number that college was less helpful in preparing them for homemaking than they believe it might have been.

The nature of the courses in home economics which were most valuable has been summarized from the replies of the women. The lack of a checking list for this question and the differences in the names of the courses which are used for purposes of description in the various institutions have made the compilation more difficult and subject to some inaccuracies.

The years of graduation and the institutions represented seem pertinent in an interpretation of the returns. In Table VIII it will be seen that very nearly one-half of the 228 were graduated in the 1915-1919 period and that slightly less than one-third completed their degrees in the post-war years, 1920-1924. One in six had a degree conferred between 1910 and 1914. Three per cent had finished college before 1910, and very nearly 5 per cent re-

TABLE VIII

YEAR OF GRADUATION FOR WOMEN TRAINED IN HOME ECONOMICS

Year	No.	Per Cent
Before 1900...........................	..	....
1900 – 1905...........................	1	.4
1905 – 1909...........................	6	2.6
1910 – 1914...........................	39	16.5
1915 – 1919...........................	97	43.4
1920 – 1924...........................	69	30.2
1925 or later.........................	11	4.7
Not given.............................	5	2.2
Total.............................	228	100.0

ceived degrees in 1925 or later. Taken as a group practically eight out of ten are graduates since 1914.

The institutions in which undergraduate and graduate work was taken number forty-three. In Table IX, Iowa State College is seen to lead in the number of its graduates who coöperated in the study. One in seven had part, if not all, of their training at Ames. One in twelve has been a student at the University of Illinois. The University of Minnesota, Ohio State University, and Purdue University have each given training to one in sixteen of the group. Kansas State Agricultural College, the University of Wisconsin, the University of Nebraska, and Michigan State College furnish approximately the same proportions. In other words, nine state institutions in the Middle West have granted degrees to 65 per cent of the 228 home economics trained women from whom data regarding the usefulness of their college courses are available.

In building curricula for prospective and present-day homemakers it would seem that courses in nutrition and dietetics might occupy a central place, for seven in ten of the group indicate that these subjects have been particularly helpful to them. Table X shows that, in order of frequency, courses in food preparation rank second, with very nearly half reporting this help. Psychology has been useful for one out of three, and only a slightly smaller per cent list clothing construction, meal planning, and home management. One in five reports chemistry and art appreciation. English, interior decoration and house planning have been particularly useful to a smaller number. Sociology, home nursing, physiology, clothing selection, literature, and education are mentioned by one in eight or ten. Among the courses listed by less than one

TABLE IX

INSTITUTIONS IN WHICH HOME ECONOMICS TRAINING WAS RECEIVED*

Name of Institution	No. of Women Attending
Iowa State College	40
Illinois, University of	22
Minnesota, University of	16
Ohio State University	16
Purdue University	16
Kansas State Agricultural College	15
Wisconsin, University of	15
Nebraska, University of	14
Michigan State College	13
New York State Teachers College, Albany	8
Kansas, University of	7
Missouri, University of	6
Oregon Agricultural College	6
Chicago, University of	5
Columbia University, Teachers College	5
Colorado Agricultural College	4
Cornell University	4
Washington, State College of	4
North Dakota State College	3
Idaho, University of	3
Kansas State Teachers College	3
Indiana, University of	3
Utah Agricultural College	3
Washington, University of	3
South Dakota State College	2
Wyoming, University of	2
†Others	18

* In several cases these women had their training in more than one institution. In those cases all institutions mentioned by them are included in the summary.
† Include Buffalo State Teachers College, University of South Dakota, Iowa State Teachers College, Rockford College, University of Maine, University of Kentucky, Lewis Institute, Florida State College for Women, Drexel Institute, Delaware, Michigan State Normal College, Simmons, Rhode Island State College, Peru State Teachers College, Montana State College, Lake Erie, Oklahoma University, Southwest State Teachers College, Phillips University, Denison, University of Maryland.

in ten are economics, child development, bacteriology, biology, design, and child care. Physics is reported by less than 4 per cent of the entire group.

For the makers of college curricula who are interested in helping to prepare women for marriage and parenthood the question that naturally arises is: to what extent do the frequencies and the lack of frequencies

· TABLE X

COURSES OF SPECIAL HELP TO HOME ECONOMICS GRADUATES

Name of Course	Number Reporting	Per Cent Reporting
Nutrition and Dietetics	158	69.3
Food Preparation	101	44.3
Psychology	76	33.3
Clothing Construction	72	31.6
Meal Planning	69	30.2
Home Management	66	29.0
Chemistry	48	21.1
Art Appreciation	44	19.2
English	37	15.7
House Planning—Interior Decoration	32	14.1
Home Nursing	26	12.1
Sociology	26	12.1
Literature	25	11.7
Physiology	25	11.7
Clothing Selection	24	11.3
Education	23	10.0
Economics	22	9.6
Child Development	22	9.6
Bacteriology	20	8.6
Biology	19	8.1
Design	18	7.7
Child Care	18	7.7
Physics	8	3.5

reported above indicate the points of emphasis that are advisable? To take but two examples, child care and physics, which come close to the end of the list, is one to assume that these courses are of little value because they are mentioned infrequently? Attention has been called in a preceding paragraph to the years of graduation for those whose replies constitute the source material of the study. In the years 1915-1925 when the majority of these women graduated there were few courses offered in the care or development of children.[2] In this case

[2] In an unpublished study of "Trends in Home Economics as shown by Catalog Offerings in 1914 and 1924," by Agnes Tilson, the statement is made that in the ten institutions studied "the ten-year period shows an increase in the interest in children. In 1914 three institutions offered cloth-

lack of mention undoubtedly points to an absence of the course rather than to a lack of usefulness. This explanation is borne out by the fact that among the needs recognized by this group more information on child training is checked by more than eight out of ten (see Table VII). The ranking of physics may be explained also by its absence from the required curriculum in many institutions. Obviously it is not fair to conclude that the importance to homemakers of courses is in proportion to the frequency with which each is listed, particularly if there has been a pronounced change in the offerings or in the content of a given course.

With an appreciation of the caution with which Tables VII and X must be used in interpreting the educational needs and helps for wives and mothers, one turns to the task of examining the findings more carefully and attempting to discover the points for emphasis in training homemakers. More information regarding the nature of the needs is available on some phases, particularly food and clothing.

Courses in Art.—Table X shows that one in five women has found general courses in art appreciation particularly helpful, and that one in seven has benefited from work in house-planning and interior decoration. A smaller proportion, one in fourteen, reported courses in design, which may have been offered either in connection with clothing or art.

ing for children; in 1924 the number increased to seven. In 1914 only one institution listed child care; in 1924 it was offered in eight institutions."

Among the schools which have offered training for leaders in the physical and mental growth of young children Merrill-Palmer School of Homemaking was the first to be developed in this country and the first students were not admitted until 1922. The policy of having children as members of the groups in home management houses was not inaugurated until the spring of 1919 at the University of Minnesota and an elective course in child training first offered at Minnesota in 1919 was one of the early developments along this line.

In addition to the listing of helpful courses there were numerous references to the appreciations which these courses had developed in the individual. A few noted the tendency which they thought their courses had had to promote expensive tastes, rather than an appreciation of the good things which might be had when ability to choose and skill in manipulation were coupled with a small expenditure of money. In many instances a knowledge of house-planning had been of practical value in securing a larger degree of comfort, convenience, and attractiveness in their own homes; in a great many cases the tendency to choose household furnishings which were beautiful and useful, instead of because they were "very popular this season," increased both the satisfaction and permanence secured from the purchase.

Table VII indicates that the same proportion, one in five, who listed courses in art in the work which had been particularly helpful wished more training in art. For all three groups, that is, including those without college degrees and those whose degrees had been granted following the completion of a major other than home economics, the percentage is the same. Thus, from the standpoint of increased appreciations and satisfactions and from that of more economical use of income, energy, and time, courses in the principles of design and the application of these principles to the selection and construction of clothing, food, furnishings and housing seem to deserve a place in the curriculum. An evaluation of existing courses in terms of their contribution to homemakers whose money incomes are limited appears to be desirable.

Courses in Child Development.—The important place which children occupy in the goals of the family and the effect which they have upon countless aspects of family life and upon the physical and mental fitness of both parents, particularly of the mother, make education in principles underlying the growth and guidance of children paramount. Throughout the entire field of training for homemaking, however, there is no phase in which courses based upon scientific findings and interpreted in terms of usefulness to present and prospective parents need to be taught with greater skill, greater understanding, or a more sane perspective. This caution is suggested at the outset because there are intimations, if not evidences, throughout the present study that in the field of human relations, whether of parent-child or husband-wife, a feeling of insecurity and of inability to handle the situations which arise may result from courses given by persons lacking a background of experience or those without a realization of the many points at which their statements and illustrations are likely to be applied—sometimes misapplied to be sure—in dealing with other individuals. In other words, the harm done by faulty information or misinterpretation in a course in art or in mathematics is likely to be less serious than that in a course dealing with the development of a human personality and his relations with others.

Table VII shows that more than eight out of ten of the home economics graduates recognize their limitations in dealing with children. For the three groups the proportion wanting more information is only slightly lower. From the data available the problems arising in connection with physical care are greatly outnumbered by those bearing upon the development of traits of personality and of abilities in the child. In other words, the process of helping several children, often with very different temperaments and degrees of ability, to reach adulthood well equipped for a relatively happy and successful life is the one for which mothers need guiding principles and increased skill.

Frequently the adjustments which are necessitated in family life by the coming of children appear to increase the difficulties. Thus it is not a lack of information regarding the plan to pursue, but a lack of time, of strength, or of money that complicates the problem for the mother. Inability to secure the coöperation of other adults may produce an insoluble problem. The need for emphasis, therefore, upon the application of principles under home conditions seems to be a consideration of no small moment if courses are to have practical value. Thus, the best nursery school, from the standpoint of training for homemaking, is the one which maintains a close association with the homes from which the children come and which provides the student with an opportunity to observe and discuss not alone the happenings in the school but those, also, of the home. If, for any one of a number of reasons, this coöperation is not possible, other methods must be employed to insure an opportunity for the individual student to see children of different ages and temperaments in home situations over a period of time. In brief, the central questions in courses in child development seem to be two: What are the basic principles underlying the process of growth and development? And how can the parent provide in the environment of the child the conditions necessary for the best development without sacrificing other members in the process?

Courses in Foods and Nutrition.—The question of what constitutes for homemakers an essential minimum of information regarding food is an interesting one. Whereas very nearly 50 per cent of the home economics group list courses in food preparation as helpful, and slightly under a third record meal planning, only one-fourth of all three groups indicate the need for more help in household skills, which was undoubtedly interpreted by the women to include the routine connected with the preparation of three meals a day. Furthermore, there is little evidence throughout the various sections of the study that food *per se* is a perplexing problem.

In Table XI the nature of the food problems encountered by the women in the three sub-groups and in the group as a whole is shown. Problems arising in connection with the establishment of good food habit in children are reported more often as a source of difficulty by the group trained in home economics than by those without it. Obviously then, skill in food preparation and a knowledge of the principles underlying it do not prevent these problems from arising. One might ask whether a knowledge of the relation of adequate food to health tends to make one over-solicitous when exceptions occur or when there is a fear that there *may* be exceptions. The plea of one young child that "we forget to talk about food today because it is Christmas" seems to point to a high degree of tension over diet in one home.

XI

NATURE OF FOOD PROBLEMS ENCOUNTERED BY WOMEN

Nature of Problem	Group A Per Cent	Group B Per Cent	Group C Per Cent	All Groups Per Cent
Food Problems with Children...............	56.4	52.0	61.3	60.4
Menu Planning..........	13.0	4.0	13.7	11.7
Food Preparation........	20.4	20.0	5.9	10.0
Food Selection...........	7.4	8.0	9.2	9.0
Economy................	3.7	4.0	8.1	7.4
Use of Time.............	3.7	12.0	5.9	5.7
No Problems Found......	14.9	12.0	15.3	15.7

For the entire group the actual preparation of food appears to cause difficulty for only one-sixth as many women as the number who record problems with the establishment of good food habits in their children. Among home economics trained persons the ratio is reduced to one in twelve, whereas it is increased to more than one in three among those who have not had similar training.

In a comparison of those having no problems in connection with the provision of food,[3] there is only a slight difference in the percentage for those without college degrees and those with majors in home economics. Since the former group are members of the longer established homes, increased experience appears to be a factor in decreasing the frequency with which problems are encountered. It is possible, also, that more practical standards are reached, thus reducing the problems.

Menu-planning, food selection, and the use of time and money are managerial phases of the provision of food for the family. In this combination one in three reports difficulty, as contrasted with the one in ten who has problems in food preparation. Among the home economics group the proportion is more than one in three; for the other two sub-groups it is more than one in four. On the basis of these figures college courses in the 1915-1925 period seem to have been less helpful in giving information on phases other than the technique of preparation. The fact that the home economics group report managerial problems in greater frequency than the other groups seems to suggest an appreciation of the importance which they attach to these matters.

A specific question asking for information regarding

[3] Only those who stated definitely that they had no problems were included. Spaces left blank were excluded in the count.

the problems of providing food for children may be responsible in part for the percentage of difficulties that was reported regarding them, but the tendency of many women to report at length on this point suggests that these problems are often a source of family tension. In the light of these facts more attention in courses to the psychic factors in diet seems warranted. The application of principles underlying habit-formation has a place in the discussions, since the belief that facts once learned will be applied skillfully in the variety of situations arising daily is not justified. Particularly does one see evidences of a lack of application when "getting the food down," because it is good for one, becomes the sole objective. The importance of psychic factors is not limited to the child, but needs to have consideration if an adequate diet is to be insured for grown members also.

The relation which good management bears to the problems of diet in connection with children has been pointed out in an earlier summary of this study.[4] The regularity with which meals are served, the physical condition of the child, the atmosphere preceding and during the meal, and the quality of food served have an important bearing upon the resultant degree of success. The degree of self-control which parents have, their agreement on policies and procedure, and the consistency with which they handle situations that arise are determining factors in the education of the child concerning diet as in other matters.

Nutrition and dietetics occupy an important place both in the training needed and that regarded as helpful. In the additional information which these homemakers feel is needed, three out of each ten in the entire group

[4] Ruth Lindquist, *A Study of Home Management in Its Relationship to Development*, pp. 60-67.

checked nutrition; in the courses which have proved most helpful seven out of ten of the home economics trained group mentioned these courses specifically. The rapid developments in the science of nutrition during the last decade make additional information seem the more necessary to those who have had some training.

Courses in Health.—There are fewer definite facts regarding the information essential for homemakers on the prevention and treatment of illness than there are on food and nutrition. A study, however, of the nature of problems which occurred in a three-year period for the 306 families included in this summary, and 49 in addition, showed that one-half of the group had one or more illnesses during that period. Operations, whooping cough, measles, and common colds were reported most frequently; constipation, diseased tonsils and adenoids, and various types of nervous diseases occurred less often. The inability to forecast the proportion of the income which is needed to promote health and the narrow margin that is left after other expenses are paid make the subject one of great importance. Training is needed which will help to keep the members of the family well, which will enable women to recognize symptoms of disease, which will promote an evaluation of activities in terms of their effect upon health, and which will promote intelligent care of members who become ill. This is particularly true for the families with moderate incomes who cannot afford to hire the additional services which become necessary if there is a lack of efficiency, endurance, or knowledge on the part of the mother. Emphasis in such courses needs to be on keeping members well and on preventing unsafe standards in the community rather than on curing disease.

Courses in Management.—Slightly less than three out of
ten have found that courses in management of the home
are helpful, and a similar proportion of those who have
had home economics training would like more information. Two out of five of those who have had majors in
departments other than home economics and one in
every two of those who are not college graduates recognize their lacks in this field.

The confusion with which the term has been used in
different institutions and by individuals makes the needs
of homemakers on this point less clear. That the ability
to use the income wisely is one of the aspects on which
help is desired is apparent, for only one in ten stated that
she had no problems of a financial nature (Table XII).
More than one in four have found it difficult to apportion
the income to the needs of the family, and one in every
six of the entire group has thought that the size of the
income made the task a more difficult one. Reference
to other economic problems is made in the selection of
food and clothing. The skill with which the income must
be managed in order to maintain a satisfactory plane of
living was noted by many. Particularly in the more recently established homes, and in those in which there
were new babies, the variation in outgo has given an uncertain basis for budgeting. One in every six reported this
problem. An inability to save and too little knowledge
of the principles which underlie the making of sound investments were another source of uncertainty. A need
for a simple and satisfactory technique of budgeting has
been recognized by more than one in ten of the entire
group; in the group without college degrees the frequency
with which this need was met was double that of those
who have had home economics training. An irregularity

in income created a problem for practically 10 per cent of the entire group and one which they did not believe they were handling satisfactorily. In a smaller number of cases the methods of securing the coöperation of the other members of the family had not been discovered.

TABLE XII

NATURE OF FINANCIAL PROBLEMS ENCOUNTERED BY WOMEN

	Group A Per Cent	Group B Per Cent	Group C Per Cent	All Groups Per Cent
Distribution of Income for Needs..............	24.2	32.0	29.4	28.7
Size of Income..........	22.6	8.0	14.9	16.4
Irregularity of Outgo.....	3.6	24.0	17.6	15.7
Saving.................	7.2	24.0	14.9	14.8
Budgeting Technique.....	18.6	12.0	9.2	11.2
Irregularity of Income....	9.3	4.0	9.7	9.3
Securing Family Cooperation..........	1.8	12.0	6.5	6.2
Finding Time............	1.8	4.0	1.2	1.7
No Problems Found......	7.2	8.0	11.7	10.3

The nature of the problems to which reference has been made in the preceding summary suggests the content of class discussions in financial management which are designed for homemakers. In addition, the collection is of value in checking against the actual needs of homemakers the subject matter which is now being presented in such courses.

In addition to the financial problems in management, there are those that grow out of a faulty use of time and energy and those which revolve about the use of leisure once it has been secured. How to provide more free time for the mother and for the group at one and the same time, and how to get the greatest amount of satisfaction from the hours away from duties are questions which cannot be answered in the same way for all people regardless of backgrounds, tastes, environments, and other factors; yet the importance of giving more time to a consideration of the use of resources which cannot always be measured in terms of dollars and cents is apparent from the replies. Limitations in income, high standards for the home, and the constancy of the responsibility for the wives and mothers tend to promote fatigue, anxiety, and some friction. To reduce the amount of each, more emphasis upon principles and their application under different types of home conditions is necessary.

Courses which encourage an evaluation of one's activities and responsibilities, whether they be in the home or in undergraduate life, would seem to have an important place. Emphasis upon the rôle of decision-maker which the individual must play throughout life if a maximum of durable satisfactions are to be secured and if one is to be able to adjust himself successfully to changing environments, provides an opportunity for relating principles of management to the experience and problems of the student.[5]

In the past the work which has been offered in management has dealt more largely with the use of money and time than with the use and development of the abilities and traits of the members of the family group— with the activities rather than with the personnel side of family life. There are suggestions throughout the replies that an understanding of human nature and of the personality traits of individuals with whom one lives and works is indispensable. In the section on courses in child development the need for more insight into the nature of children has been brought out. In the development of curricula increased attention may well be paid to this

---

[5] In this connection see Margaret Mead, *Growing Up in Samoa*, chap. XIV.

phase of training for marriage and parenthood. In other words, in home management as in industrial management, efficiency which takes account only of the inanimate material with which one works is likely to fall far short of being *good* management. The comment of one woman suggests the need of relating the principles underlying human relations to the student and her problems, if the foundation for harmony in family life is successfully laid. The lack of help and of interest in problems of personal adjustment during her period of formal education has made the direction of family life far more difficult for her.

Courses in Textiles and Clothing.—The training which these women have had in clothing has been of more frequent help in the making of garments and of furnishings than it has in selection, if one observes the summary of the helps found in Table X. As in the case of foods, the courses available in the period preceding 1925 help to explain the emphasis which the group places upon this phase.[6] For the most part the offerings dealt with the teaching of skills in hand and machine work. The selection of fabrics and of designs was brought in chiefly as preparatory to problems of construction. The discussion of the economics of clothing was more likely to be incidental. There is undoubtedly another reason why con-

[6] In an unpublished study of "Trends in Home Economics as shown by Catalog Offerings of 1914 and 1924," by Agnes Tilson, courses in clothing appearing in the upper quartile are as follows:

	(Millinery	Embroidery Basketry		(Millinery
1914	(Dressmaking	Crafts		(Textiles
	(Sewing	Adv. Dressmaking	1924	(History of Costume
	(Textiles	Domestic Laundry		(Dressmaking
		Drafting and Dress Design		(Clothes for Children
		Handwork		(Elem. Dress Design
		Elementary clothing		(Advanced Dressmaking

struction courses are listed by one out of every three women. When there are available time and energy, coupled with a fair degree of skill, the homemaker's contribution to the money income of the family by the making of garments and furnishings is likely to be considerable. In other words, these women recognize that ability of this type acquired in college courses has often been a means of stretching the income.

In a comparison of the nature of problems existing among the three groups of women (Table XIII), construction is listed by but one in twelve for the group as a whole and by one in thirteen for those who have had home economics training. More pronounced are the difficulties arising in the selection of clothing. More than one in three of all the groups have found that the rapid growth of children before apparel is nearly worn out complicates both the use of money and of time. An inability to prolong the period over which garments can be worn is partly a matter of having available too few easily altered designs. A lack of standardization in sizes necessitates

TABLE XIII

NATURE OF CLOTHING PROBLEMS ENCOUNTERED BY WOMEN

	Group A Per Cent	Group B Per Cent	Group C Per Cent	All Groups Per Cent
Sizes*...................	33.4	44.0	38.1	37.8
Economy...............	28.0	36.0	20.6	23.2
Durability..............	18.6	8.0	20.1	19.0
Selection...............	26.0	16.0	15.7	18.0
Adequate Time.........	1.8	8.0	11.7	9.3
Construction...........	9.3	12.0	7.7	8.7
Laundering†............	1.8	....	9.6	7.7
Guidance of Children.....	5.6	....	5.1	4.9
No Problems Found......	7.4	4.0	11.7	9.5

* This refers particularly to the problems of out-growing garments before they are worn out and to the lack of standardization in children's apparel.
† Particularly shrinking and fading.

the expenditure of more time and energy in buying and a futile effort to use devices other than shopping-in-person. This is particularly true in the purchase of children's apparel.

To one in five of the home economics group helps in economy are needed; for those without college degrees the ratio is slightly higher than one in four, while for the smaller group who are college graduates with a major other than home economics it is above one in three. Lack of durability, closely associated with economy, is a source of concern for one in five of the entire group. General questions relating to selection, including design, fabrics, the amount to be allotted for different items, and knowing what to get for the children in the next stages, are found more frequently in the group without college degrees where the ratio is one in four. For the three groups taken together the figure is slightly less than one in five. It is interesting to note that the home economics group has problems of laundering more often than problems of construction, and also that the difficulty of securing time for sewing and mending appears very much more frequently than in either of the other groups.

An additional problem which is found only occasionally is that of encouraging the older children—particularly those of adolescent age—of the family to select suitable clothing and to be satisfied with the amount and the quality which are within the family income. Because there were few families in the groups with older children the real extent of the problem and the need for help cannot be gauged. There is evidence to support the belief that this question is one which is closely associated with the type of plan that is made for using the income. In homes where family finances are an occasion for group discussion there seem to be fewer charges by the children of having less than they need.

In a summary of the information relating to clothing which is contained in the study, the fact that but one in ten of the entire group reported no problems indicates the need for focusing attention upon courses in clothing which are based upon research data. To teach one to make garments is no longer sufficient. Rather the central questions become: what constitutes good management in the handling of present-day clothing problems and how can consumers help to insure a wiser use of their time and income? Does the profit motive in industry and business deplete the allotment for this item of expenditure through the appeals made by advertisers without giving value received? If so, what recourse do the heads of families have? To what extent is the education of the consumer possible and desirable in an economic order that is highly dynamic?

The tendency in the building of courses in clothing in a limited number of institutions has been summarized by Agnes Tilson as follows:

Of the 41 new courses in the 1924 offerings, 10 were food subjects, 26 were clothing subjects and 5 were household administration. Does this mean that there was a greater effort on the part of clothing faculties to hold their place in the curriculum or does it mean that there is a greater demand from the public for help in personal appearance than for information about nutrition and the business of the home? However, with this increased time for clothing, it is interesting to note that there is not a corresponding increase in the directing of the buying of ready-made clothing and in caring for clothing.[7]

[7] An unpublished study of "Trends in Home Economics as shown by Catalog Offerings of 1914 and 1924."

If this trend be true in other institutions, one might well ask how greatly such courses will function in modern homemaking.

Courses in Related Sciences.—Of the courses in related sciences which have been helpful in homemaking, psychology is listed by one in three of the home economics group. In the training which is needed it ranks second and is checked by more than one half of the three groups. Thus it appears that there is a keen appreciation on the part of the women that an understanding of human nature will go far in helping them to solve their problems.

For one in five, courses in chemistry have been particularly helpful. In the light of the number of hours that have been required in chemistry in many departments of home economics, the question of its relative value for those who are interested primarily in homemaking, and not in positions as technicians or research workers, seems a relevant one for builders of curricula.

With the exceptions of psychology and chemistry, related sciences are seldom mentioned as a special help. Whether this omission is due to relative importance when compared with other more closely connected courses, whether the subject matter is less essential for homemaking than for other fields of work which graduate students enter, or whether the methods of presentation used are less effective than others would be, one cannot say. The replies do lead one to ask whether there may not be a need for a more careful analysis of required courses in terms of value, inasmuch as the old doctrine of transfer of training is no longer a justification for some of the work that was at one time prescribed in the interests of disciplinary value.

Sociology, physiology, education, economics, bacteriol-

ogy, biology, and physics are in the class of the infrequently needed courses for homemaking, if one is to judge
by the returns from this study. In no one of these does
mention of its usefulness occur by more than one in eight
of the home economics trained women, and physics is
relegated to the position of the least needed since but 3.5
per cent refer to it. Before passing judgment on the place
which these courses should occupy in a curriculum for
homemaking, it is necessary to find out how many of them
have been taken by a representative sample of women now
in their homes and the reasons why subjects which appear to have unusual usefulness have shown so little relation to the conduct of a household. Certainly there is
a need for much more information on the subject matter which should be included in required courses. There
is also a need for an integration of the various units and
improved methods of teaching.

Electives.—Figures on the elective courses which this
group of women has found most helpful are not available. English and literature are mentioned by more than
one in ten, and there are several who comment on the
pleasure which an appreciation of music has afforded.
With the change in the routine of the household and the
increase in leisure which is approaching, even if it has not
yet been secured, there is need for women who direct
family life to have acquired interests in things apart from
techniques and skills in homemaking. These hobbies,
if they are not dropped nor followed too intensively,
make the woman a more interested and interesting member in groups within and outside of the family. In addition, such adjustments as those occasioned when the children leave home, when they marry, and when deaths

occur are made more successfully if there are still things in life to which one can look forward.

In this period of pre-marriage training there is need for an appreciation on the part of administrators and instructors that not all of the women enrolled in courses will marry, and that some may not have any choice in the matter. If the emphasis is placed too largely upon marriage as the one career for women, it is less likely that those who do not marry will succeed in finding a niche into which they may fit with satisfaction to themselves and others. With some, the feeling that they have been cheated out of life's richest experience and the only career worth having, will result in cynicism and bitterness. The prevention, in so far as possible, of the period of maladjustment that is likely to come with the realization that the probability of marriage has passed, should be one of the tasks of those who provide training for family life. *Conclusions.*—In the preceding section the replies have been summarized and interpreted in terms of the assistance given through courses. But there is another extremely important type of help which the period of college training can give, and this seems to many of the home economics group to outweigh the subject matter presented. There are numerous tributes to the instructors whom these women have had as students. The benefits which they secured in their late teens and early twenties from contacts with mature minds, able leaders, and well-poised personalities have enlarged their concept of the possibilities of homemaking and have strengthened the desire to construct for themselves a philosophy of life which will withstand discouragement and trial. For the most part, often unconsciously, college has provided the student in out-of-classroom hours with some of the most enduring of values. For some, circumstances have made possible many of such associations; for others they have been very limited. In the light of such statements it would seem that in training for marriage and parenthood the selection of the faculty, the provision for student-faculty contacts, the atmosphere created by the members of the teaching and administrative corps, and the size of the classes are all of very special importance.

Education is no longer regarded as a process which can be completed in high school or college. On the contrary, homemakers find that family life, viewed through the eyes of a wife and mother, presents many situations for which they had not recognized the need of training before marriage. As a result, they turn to various facilities which provide a part of this information. If study classes or lectures in child development are not available in their locality, they depend upon books, magazines, and bulletins to help them; if study classes are available, literature seems to be used in increasing quantity. In a summary of the reading that is done by the entire group, more than half of the books reported are on the subject of child care and development.

The various agencies in the community to which the homemaker looks for guidance, or which she helps to develop in response to her needs, are discussed in Chapter VIII. From the viewpoint of those who are considering the training to be given for marriage and parenthood, the list is an interesting one, for in it one sees the necessity of making plans not alone for the period of pre-marriage and pre-parental training. The very nature of family life and of the sciences which contribute to its success, because they are not static, make education in homemaking a lifelong process. If the education is wisely directed there cannot be too much of it. Programs need to be devised for rural groups quite as much as for those in cities, but to be really useful they must be based on the needs of the individual group. Many study outlines are most valuable when they are used as a point of departure, the direction of the departure depending upon the problems that are uppermost in the minds of the group.

In the following chapter, catalog offerings of the nine institutions in which 65 per cent of the home economics group have been enrolled are analyzed, with a view to determining how largely present curricula meet the needs that have been recognized by these homemakers. The findings are presented for those who are builders of curricula.

CHAPTER VII

PRESENT TRENDS IN COLLEGE TRAINING FOR MARRIAGE AND PARENTHOOD

A COMPREHENSIVE STUDY of present trends in college training for marriage and parenthood would include an analysis of all courses which relate either directly or indirectly to appreciations of marriage in any or all of its aspects and to the acquisition of ability in promoting stable and successful family life. In addition to an examination of the offerings for students majoring in home economics, it would investigate all of the offerings, both required and elective, in such departments as those of sociology, economics, English, philosophy, and in the professional schools. The attitudes of the faculty on marriage and family life would be ascertained, for here, as in other instances, the supposedly indirect training often has the most direct and permanent influence on the thinking and acting of individuals. In the absence of such a study and with the difficulties that stand in the way of making it, a more limited survey has been made. From the catalogs of the nine colleges and universities[1] in which 65 per cent of the home economics group considered in these chapters had their training, the present offerings in home economics and allied subjects have been studied. A comparison of these offerings with the educational needs and helps which have already been summarized from the comments of the group is the subject of this chapter.

[1] These are the Universities of Illinois, Minnesota, Nebraska, Ohio, Purdue, and Wisconsin and the State Colleges of Iowa, Kansas, and Michigan. Announcements for 1929-30 were used in all but two cases. The 1927-28 was the only edition available in the one and in the other the issue was that for 1930-1931.

The first trend away from the earlier policy in departments of home economics which one notes is that of specialization.   Instead of one curriculum through a period of four years for all students who enter a department of home economics, there are several.   In one institution but five are presented, while in another there are fifteen clearly defined lines of interest from which one may choose.   The descriptive statements contained in the catalogs make clear that education for earning is one of the primary aims of each department and that the basis for setting up special requirements within a department or division is a vocational one.   Thus one student may prefer to be qualified upon graduation for institutional management, while another will wish to enter the field of textiles and clothing in order to prepare herself as a buyer or as a research worker.   In the nine institutions there are prescribed courses which all students must complete regardless of their vocational plans.   It is these requirements[2] that are summarized in Table XIV.

The emphasis placed upon training for homemaking *per se* appears to vary considerably.   In one of the nine curricula certain courses beyond those required of all students in the department are prescribed for those who take a major in homemaking or home management; in the remainder there is a policy which permits very great freedom in electives.   From the brief description of the departments in the catalogs, the degree to which special provision is made for preparing college graduates to enter upon homemaking is gleaned.   The following statements show the variation:

[2] In one of these the entire course which is prescribed for homemaking is summarized; in two others it is the general major, though in each of these two institutions there is also a separate general course prescribed as a basis for professional majors.   This latter curriculum is not included in the summary.

"One important aim of the Department of Home Economics is to educate young women for the responsibility of homemaking. All women have homemaking responsibilities even though they do not marry. Inasmuch as eighty per cent of college graduates become homemakers, opportunity to receive adequate preparation for this responsibility is given. . . . The following courses in Home Economics are planned to meet the need of:

> Those students who desire survey courses in Home Economics in preparation for homemaking or as a part of their cultural education.

> Those students who wish a broader and a deeper knowledge of the sciences and the arts pertaining to the home. . . ."[3]

"The plan of study in home economics has two functions: to give to the student training which will fit her to become a responsible citizen and an intelligent homemaker and housekeeper; to train her for a skilled occupation by which she may become self-supporting."[4]

"The curricula in home economics are designed to train young women in homemaking and for a payroll job in which all or most of them engage for at least a short period. Throughout the training period there are a certain number and kind of courses required to safeguard the preparation for homemaking. The first two years are essentially the same for all students irrespective of later specialization for the payroll job."[5]

"This major is planned for students who do not wish to be trained in the professional home economics majors; and

[3] *Bulletin of the University of Nebraska, College of Agriculture Announcements 1929-1930*, pp. 23, 67.
[4] *Bulletin of Purdue University*, Vol. XXX, No. 7, p. 145.
[5] *Bulletin of the University of Minnesota*, Vol. XXXI, No. 28, p. 37.

therefore is less severely technical and allows a more liberal choice of electives."⁶

"The courses given in this department are planned primarily to meet the needs of students who desire a knowledge of the general principles and facts of home economics. Opportunity is given through elective courses in the third and fourth years to emphasize various phases of home economics such as household and institutional management, nutrition and dietetics, house planning and furnishing, and textiles, clothing, and costume design. Courses in the teaching of home economics are available for those who plan to teach."⁷

"The requirements for the first two years of this curriculum are the same for all students. In the third and fourth years they may elect courses which contribute to special preparation for the many fields that are open to home economics graduates. It is possible to secure training . . . for homemaking itself."⁸

SUMMARY OF PRESENT-DAY CURRICULA

An analysis of the general curricula in these nine institutions is of particular interest in indicating the courses which are now being stressed. The summary in Table XIV has been prepared in percentages rather than in numbers of hours because some of the institutions were on the quarter system and others on the semester plan. In addition to knowledge of the types of subject matter required, information regarding the specific courses available helps to reveal existing opportunities. The use of different titles in the different institutions prevents absolute accuracy in such a summary, but a careful reading of descriptions has minimized error. In Table XV these results are presented.

⁶ *Bulletin of the University of Wisconsin*, Gen'l Series, No. 1357, Series No. 1583, Home Economics Courses 1929-30, p. 25.

⁷ *University of Illinois Bulletin*, Vol. XXVII, No. 27, p. 136.

⁸ *Ohio State University Bulletin*, Vol. XXXIII, No. 15, p. 41.

TABLE XIV

SUMMARY OF GENERAL CURRICULA IN NINE DEPARTMENTS OF HOME ECONOMICS

1927-31

	No. of Institutions Reporting Required Courses	Range in Per Cent of Total Curriculum	Average Per Cent for Institutions Requiring Courses	Average Per Cent
Home Economics				
Foods and Nutrition....	9	2.5–12.2	6.8	
Textiles and Clothing...	9	4.2–10.6	5.8	
Art..................	8	2.5– 6.8	3.7	
Housing and Equipment	7	2.3– 5.2	3.6	
Management.........	8	2.3– 6.0	3.0	
Child Development.....	6	1.6– 3.3	2.4	
Health (excluding personal hygiene)....	4	1.6– 2.6	2.1	
Required electives—not specifically named....	3	3.3– 7.7	5.0	
Seminar in Home Economics..........	6	....	...	
All Home Economics....	9	23.3–37.9	...	27
*Physical Sciences**				
Chemistry............	8	8. –11.7	9.4	
Zoology..............	5†	2.6– 4.0	3.5	
Botany..............	2†	2.6– 3.9	3.2	
Physiology...........	6	2.0– 3.9	2.7	
Physics..............	5	2.0– 3.0	2.5	
Bacteriology..........	6	2.0– 2.6	2.4	
*Social Sciences**				
Psychology...........	6	2.0– 8.0	3.6	
History..............	4	1.6– 5.3	3.2	
Economics...........	5	2.3– 4.0	3.1	
Sociology............	6	1.6– 4.2	2.3	
*Other Courses**				
English, Literature, and Public Speaking......	9	4.7–10.0	8.2	
Electives within a prescribed group.....	5	4.6– 8.3	6.6	
Modern Language......	2	5.5– 6.6	6.0	
Physical Education.....	6‡	1.0– 3.2	1.9	
Personal Hygiene.......	7	.6– 1.5	.9	
Open (Non-prescribed) Electives.............	9	1.7–43.0	...	22

* In one institution (Nebraska) 14.4 per cent of the course is made up of electives from the physical sciences, 12 per cent from the social sciences, and 3.2 from "appreciation" courses.
† In two of these institutions there is a choice permitted of zoology or botany.
‡ In two additional institutions courses in physical education are required but they do not carry credit.

TABLE XV
NATURE OF COURSE OFFERINGS WITH FREQUENCY OF REQUIREMENT
FOR GRADUATION*

	No. Listing	No. Requiring
Art		
Principles of Design	9	8
Costume Design	7	2
Appreciation and History†	4	2
Crafts	5	.
Advanced Design	2	.
Drawing	2	1
Child Development		
Child Care and Development	9	6
Development of Older Children	1	.
Special Problems	3	.
The Child in the Home†	2	.
Foods and Nutrition		
Principles of Preparation	9	9
Principles of Nutrition	9	6
Food Buying	6	4
Diet in Health	7	3
Nutrition of Children	6	1
Diet in Disease	5	1
Home Project in Foods	3	3
Food Management	1	1
Food Preparation—Meal Planning†	4	.
Experimental Cookery	7	.
Quantity Cookery	8	.
Special Problems in Foods	4	.
Camp Cookery†	3	.
Preservation of Foods	1	.
Nutrition Classes	2	.
Health		
Personal Health	7	7
Family Health	7	4
Public Health	1	1
Health of Children	1	.
First Aid and Physical Diagnosis	1	.
Housing and Equipment		
Home Planning	8	7
Interior Decoration and House Furnishings	9	4
Household Equipment	4	2
Special Problems	4	.
Household Electrical Equipment	1	.
Housing†	1	.
Home Management		
Home Management	9	8
Home Management Residence	9	6

* Only the courses which are required and those which seem to be directly related to home-making are included.
† These courses have been designed primarily as elective courses for students in other departments, including liberal arts, nursing, social work, forestry, and engineering.

TABLE XV (*Continued*)

	No. Listing	No. Requiring
Selection of Clothing and Furnishings......	2	1
Special Problems......................	3	..
Elements of Home Management†..........	2	.
Economic and Social Problems...........	1	.
Textiles and Clothing		
Textiles.............................	9	8
Principles of Construction...............	9	7
Home Project.........................	3	3
Clothing Selection†....................	5	2
Advanced Clothing.....................	5	2
Special Problems......................	5	1
Textile or Clothing Economics...........	4	1
Principles of Pattern Structure...........	2	1
Millinery.............................	4	.
History of Costume....................	4	.
Clothing and Textile Industry...........	2	.
Advanced Textiles.....................	3	.
Children's Clothing....................	2	.
Hygiene of Clothing....................	1	.
Survey of Home Economics.................	6	6
Psychology		
General..............................	9	6
Childhood and Adolescence..............	3	2
The Psychology of Leadership...........	1	1
Advanced Child Psychology.............	1	.
Economics		
Principles............................	9	5
Household or Consumption Economics.....	4	1
Consumers' Marketing..................	1	.
Sociology		
Introductory Course...................	9	6
The Modern Family....................	2	1
The Community and the Child...........	1	1
European Family Life..................	1	.
Field Work in Social Service.............	2	.
Community Organization................	1	.
Social Problems.......................	1	.

As is seen from Table XIV there is a wide range in the proportion of the entire curriculum which falls within the department of home economics. In one institution the required amount is less than one-fourth of the total credit hours; in five it is between one-fourth and one-third, and in three it is over one-third. For the group as a whole the average is 27 per cent. There is also a variation in the number of electives for which students may register. In one institution where courses are prescribed through the four years for those desiring to major in homemaking only 1.7 per cent of the courses taken before graduation are taken upon the choice of the student; in four the per cent is approximately one-fourth; in three the ratio varies from one in four to one in three, while in one, freedom is given in more than four out of every ten hours. The average for the nine institutions is 22 per cent. The remainder of the curriculum is made up of courses in the physical and social sciences together with those in the arts. These are stressed in varying degrees by different institutions.

Offerings and Requirements in Home Economics.—Both in point of time and in the number of institutions requiring them, courses in foods and nutrition and in textiles and clothing rank first and second respectively for home economics subject matter. Courses in art, housing and equipment, and management are listed among those required in all but one or two of the institutions. Each of these three comprises a smaller portion of the entire curriculum than does foods or clothing. In only six institutions are there required courses in child development, though they are offered in all of the nine departments. Courses in personal hygiene are required in seven institutions, while those in health of the family must be taken in only four of the nine. Three other departments offer courses in family health. In three institutions a part of the courses permits a choice within the home economics field and each prescribes only the number of hours which must be selected from a more or less varied list.

A more detailed study of the nature of the offerings in home economics, both required and elective, throws additional light on the present trends. In foods and nutrition, "Principles of Food Preparation" is the only course which is everywhere required. In two-thirds of the institutions, "Principles of Nutrition" must be taken before graduation. "Food-Buying" and "Economics of the Food Supply," offered either as a separate course or as a unit in another, is now required in four institutions, while it is offered in two additional departments. "Diet in Health" and a "Home Project in Foods" constitute a part of the required curriculum in three institutions. In only one university are "Nutrition of Children" and "Food Management" prescribed; in another institution, "Diet in Disease" must be taken. In Table XV are listed other offerings in sections of Foods and Nutrition, but in no instance are any of these required.

In Textiles and Clothing, the courses in "Textiles" and in "Principles of Construction" appear to be more important than any of the others. A "Home Project in Clothing" is required by three institutions. Two require completion of courses in "Clothing Selection" and "Advanced Clothing." A "Special Problems" course, one in "Textile or Clothing Economics," and one in "Principles of Pattern Structure," are each prescribed in one institution. Among the offerings in this section "Children's Clothing" is listed twice.

"Principles of Design" occurs most frequently both among the offerings and the requirements in art. "Costume Design" and "Art Appreciation" are each required in two institutions. "Crafts," "Advanced Design," and "Drawing" constitute additional offerings.

Among the courses in housing and equipment there is no one course which is required in all institutions. "House Planning" is found more frequently than any other with "Interior Decoration and Furnishings" having second place. In two institutions "Household Equipment" is prescribed. This course in the four departments which offer it deals with selection and efficiency primarily, rather than with the artistic aspects.

A discussion course in the use of the family's resources is the one in management which appears most frequently among those required. Residence in a home management house, although offered in all of the institutions, is required in but six of them. In three[9] the presence of an infant or a young child provides a setting for teaching child care and development under conditions approximating those of a home, thus giving an opportunity for relating principles of management to child development. While there are a few other courses listed, the two mentioned above are generally regarded as the college courses in management.

A general course in the physical and mental growth of the pre-school child is the one which is both offered and required most frequently. There is no institution without such a course, and in seven,[10] nursery schools provide opportunity for observation and some assistance as part of the course. With the exception of one institution there is none that describes courses promoting an understanding of the school child. In two institutions,

[9] A. E. Richardson and M. L. Miller, *Child Development and Parental Education in Home Economics*, p. 84.
[10] *Ibid.*, p. 83.

however, a course in the psychology of childhood and adolescence divides the time given to a consideration of the younger and the older child.

Offerings and Requirements in the Physical Sciences.— Among the physical sciences, chemistry easily claims first place, making up, as it does, from 8 to 12 per cent of the entire curriculum in eight institutions. Zoölogy and botany are required less frequently and in smaller quantities. Physiology, physics, and bacteriology, although they are required in more institutions, each makes up less than 3 per cent of the curriculum, or approximately one-fourth as much as chemistry.

Offerings and Requirements in the Social Sciences.—In the social sciences it is psychology which shows the highest percentage of the general curriculum, but the average for the six institutions in which it is required is considerably less than half of that provided by courses in chemistry. In addition to general psychology, offerings include "Children and Adolescence," required by two departments, the "Psychology of Leadership," and "Advanced Child Psychology." Economics is another of the social sciences in which at least one course is required by five departments; in four departments a course in the "Economics of Consumption" is designed especially for home economics majors, and in one, "Consumer's Marketing" has recently been added.

There is greater range in the number of courses in sociology than in economics, although in this field, as in economics, the requirement is largely that of an introductory course. In only one institution is a course in "The Family" made a requirement and, in another, "The Community and the Child" must be taken. The additional courses that are listed in sociology are in the nature of offerings rather than of requirements. History is a part of the requirement in four institutions, and it ranges from 1.6 per cent of the curriculum in one instance to 5.3 per cent in another.

Other Offerings and Requirements.—A fourth type of subject matter includes English, modern languages, physical education, personal hygiene, and certain electives within prescribed lists. Turning again to Table XIV English, literature, and public speaking will be found to approach, but not equal, chemistry in the emphasis that is placed upon the group. In only two institutions are languages required, though in several they are found in a list of electives from which a choice must be made. Physical education is required in eight of the institutions, usually throughout the first two years.

A COMPARISON OF OFFERINGS AND REQUIREMENTS WITH
NEEDS AND HELPS OF HOMEMAKERS

This summary of offerings and requirements helps one to view present-day curricula from the standpoint of the training that they provide for marriage and parenthood. The needs and the helps reported by married alumnae of the nine institutions studied, together with those of thirty-four other institutions, have been presented in the preceding chapter.[11] A comparison of the curricula with these recognized needs and helps leads to some interesting and thought-provoking observations.

Children, Their Care and Development.—Child training is the subject about which more than three-quarters of the mothers feel the need of more information. The question of how much useful knowledge can be provided in the pre-parental period of study has not yet been an-

[11] See Tables VII, X, XI, XII, XIII.

swered, but it would seem that principles underlying child behavior and their application might develop appreciations, standards, insight, and some skills. Whether the policy of prescribing definite courses is a wiser one than merely offering a range of subject matter and permitting a maximum of choice has not been determined. At present, however, the trend seems to be in the direction of requiring those courses without which the faculty believes the student would be poorly equipped. If this tendency is a desirable one or if there is no system of faculty advisers, it would seem that at least as much emphasis should be placed upon essentials of child development as upon essentials in food preparation. While nine institutions offer courses in both subjects, and all require the course in foods, only two-thirds prescribe courses in child development. Apparently seven of these institutions provide for actual contacts with children through nursery schools, home management houses, or both.

Additional subject matter dealing with children is found in other departments, but the number offering courses in the nutrition of children, clothing problems, psychology of childhood and adolescence, and the needs of older children is limited. One wonders, too, how much attention is paid in housing and furnishings courses to the needs of families with children and in management courses to managerial problems arising in connection with children. In one institution a required course in "The Community and the Child" is described as follows:

The family as a social institution, its historical development and present status. Modern conditions affecting home life. The child as affected by economic and social factors out-

side the home. The dependent and the neglected child. Social legislation affecting the child. Social responsibility toward
the child.[12]

Although an overcrowded curriculum may make the
requirement of such a course unwise, it would seem that
its content ought to place it among the list of suggested
electives in every institution.

Psychology.—More than half of this group of wives and
mothers desire more help in psychology. In this respect
one-third of the home economics women have found
their college training particularly helpful. As has been
pointed out, the present curricula of six institutions prescribe between 2 and 8 per cent in this department, and all
provide a range of electives. Perhaps it is fair to raise
the questions of how closely some courses in psychology
are related to the needs of the individual student and how
constructive the material of the courses is. In other words,
does the general course enable one to understand human
nature without losing respect for it and does it provide
help in maintaining harmonious human relations?   In
a few instances, comments of the women suggest the
need for more knowledge regarding "the psychology of
men."

Courses in the psychology of childhood and adolescence are prescribed in two institutions in which child development is required in addition. In one institution a
course in the psychology of leadership is required. In
connection with the offerings in this field, yet apart from
them, is the freshman requirement in several institutions,
designed to help the student adjust herself to a new environment and to enable her to choose a career in which
she may earn a livelihood most happily and successfully.

[12] *Ohio State University Bulletin*, Vol. XXXIII, No. 15, p. 126.

Home Management.—Home management ranks third in frequency among the types of additional training in which the women feel the need of help. More than one in four of the home economics group have found the courses which they have had particularly helpful in their homemaking. As has already been indicated, at least two courses are now offered in all of the institutions, and there is a tendency to require both of them in the general major. The length of the laboratory or residence course varies from five days in one institution to twelve weeks in another. There is also a variation in the number of students living in the house at one time, which affects the length of the experience per student. Without more information there is no way of knowing the extent to which the students in residence carry the managerial responsibilities nor the degree of freedom and encouragement they are given in making decisions; yet the importance of having the resident instructor serve as an adviser, rather than as the manager, is apparent if the period of training is to be most profitable. It is this distinction in the function of the instructor that is likely to make of many potential home management houses merely practice houses. More information is also needed before one can determine how much training is provided in the use of the human resources of the group and in the application of the principles underlying harmonious relationships.

Comments of some of the women who have had courses in home management residence stress the need of maintaining reasonable standards if the course is to be both useful and encouraging to prospective homemakers. If housekeeping, food preparation, the care of young children, or hospitality is made to seem exceedingly difficult, fatiguing, and time-consuming, the incentive to have a home of one's own is lessened. In addition, the scale of values becomes one which must be entirely readjusted under home conditions. The actual training in home management and in a philosophy of family life which could have been given in such a course is thereby greatly reduced.

In the comments of both the men and the women there is frequently a tendency to indicate that the management of the home is the sphere of the wife while that of the husband is earning the income. In a group of families that is made up so largely of home economics graduates, it would be interesting to know whether a major in home economics tends to divide the responsibilities assumed by husband and wife more completely and whether instructors in management and child development quite unconsciously magnify the position of the woman to a degree that interferes with joint planning and sharing. *Nutrition.*—Very nearly one-third of the women wish more training in nutrition, and seven in ten of the home economics group regard the courses in nutrition and dietetics which they have had as exceedingly helpful for homemaking. In this respect existing curricula appear to meet the need, if one can judge by the titles and catalog descriptions. All of the institutions offer at least one course in "Principles of Nutrition," and there are seven that list a separate course in "Diet in Health" or Dietetics. Neither of these, however, is a requirement in all of the institutions that list them. In many of the departments there are one or more additional courses. For example, one college affords an opportunity for nutrition classes among children. In some of the others help in menu-planning and serving of children in the nursery school is given by the students.

Household Skills.—Only one in four of the entire group reports the need of more help in the household skills. In the home economics group very nearly one-half regard the training received in courses in food preparation as particularly helpful; slightly less than one-half record courses in clothing construction. In the light of these figures it would seem that a knowledge and application of principles are desirable in the curriculum. Whether the amount of time now given to these phases is a minimum or more nearly a maximum remains a question, but the wide range in the requirement suggests the desirability of further study on this point. In several institutions there is a tendency to require a home project in both foods and clothing as a means of increasing the student's experience in other than college hours. One finds also the policy of providing for electives from which the student may choose both in terms of interests and needs. It is interesting to discover, too, that in several institutions students who have had accredited courses in high school are required to take fewer courses in foods and clothing in college, thus increasing the number of electives for which they may register.

The extent to which managerial problems in foods and clothing have arisen in these homes leads one to desire more information regarding the emphasis that is placed upon these aspects of foods and clothing in the beginning courses. A freshman course or unit in textiles is in keeping with the training needed for homemaking, particularly if selection and care of fabrics are given an important place. It becomes less useful for this purpose if it deals largely with microscopic studies, textile designs, and the evolution of the textile industry. Economics of clothing and clothing selection are much less frequently offered or required than is the course in principles of construction, yet the selection and the cost of ready-to-wear garments is one of the problems of the modern home. The lack of time for sewing and the strain that it brings, which are reported by many women, lead one to ask how largely training can develop skill and teach short cuts and whether the wiser plan is to spend a larger amount of the training period in a study of ready-to-wear articles and commercial agencies that provide the family with clothing. Possibly it is with this shift of emphasis in mind that the faculties of two institutions do not require courses in clothing construction.

Among the offerings in the study or preparation of foods the proportion of emphasis upon selection and other managerial problems is seen. Four institutions require courses or units in food buying and economic aspects of food, but nine require principles of preparation, thus intimating that knowledge of how to prepare is more important than how to buy. In addition to food buying one institution also requires food management which is described as follows:

Determination and study of the management factors involved in the food problems of the homemaker.[13]

Art.—More training in art is desired by one in five of the entire group, but the nature of the training is not indicated. From the comments of the home economics group an opportunity to gain an appreciation of art has been valued by one in five. Unless the courses in design provide this adequately, only four institutions are now affording such training through courses in art appreciation. It may well be, however, that this is one of the cases

[13] *The Bulletin of the University of Minnesota*, Vol. XXXI, No. 28, p. 67.

in which good teaching and well-selected illustrative material in the other courses in art lessen the need for a separate unit in appreciation.

House planning, interior decoration, and home furnishings, which are usually regarded as a part of the fine or applied art department, have been helpful to one in seven of the home economics group. At the present time no one of these is required in the curriculum of the nine institutions; in one institution there is no course listed in house planning. One department lists planning and equipment of a home under home management. The person who gives the course is one whose training enables her to build up in the students an appreciation of the principles of design and color. The description of this course as it appears in the catalog is as follows:

> Study of the small house which aims at more intelligent planning in building and furnishing. House plans, kitchen arrangements, and equipment of house studied from homemaker's point of view of economy, convenience, and beauty.[14]

Such a course would seem to aid the student immeasurably in finding happiness in standards within the reach of a small or moderate income. In a day when more than half of the families rent the dwellings in which they live, and remodeling is largely out of their control, knowledge of standards for selection becomes increasingly important. The comments of some of the group regarding courses in art indicate that training occasionally tends to establish expensive tastes.

Philosophy and Literature.—Thus far only the further training desired and the courses of particular help in home economics and in psychology have been compared

[14] *Ibid.*

with present catalog offerings and requirements. Philosophy and literature are additional subjects about which one in four of the entire group would like more knowledge. Aside from the courses in English composition, argumentation, and public speaking, which make up the major part of the requirement shown in Table XIV, and the opportunity for free electives, there is no provision for these courses. A study of registrations would be necessary before one would know how generally they are being elected by students in departments of home economics.

Sociology and Economics.—More sociology and more economics are desired by approximately one in five women. One in eight of the home economics group has found her courses in sociology of special help, while economics has seemed useful to one in ten. Even at the present time, when more attention is being paid to the social sciences, only a part of the institutions require courses in these fields. In a day when the direction of a household is so closely related to institutions, groups, and agencies outside the home, a lack of knowledge regarding the setting and the conditions in the midst of which family life must be conducted, is a handicap. From the viewpoint of the community, training that is focused too largely upon the individual family and one's obligations to a single home is likely to develop but little social interest and responsibility. It is possible that past training has been somewhat remiss in this respect.

Courses, however, are but one requisite. Quite as important are instructors who are able to evaluate their subject matter in terms of the needs of the homemaker and who can secure the sustained interest of the students. Frequently the fact that closely related courses appear remote from present-day problems limits their background and usefulness.

Physical Sciences.—The offerings in the physical sciences remain to be compared with the help which they have provided for homemaking. One wonders if chemistry, which is mentioned by but one in five of the home economics group, should continue to make up from 8 to 12 per cent of the general curriculum. Physiology, bacteriology, biology, and physics, though reported as particularly useful by between 4 and 12 per cent of the group, are required much less frequently and in smaller amounts than chemistry, so that the judgments of a past generation of home economics graduates are less significant on this point.

There appears to be a need in the physical, as in the social, sciences for an evaluation of the factual material to be incorporated in courses designed for homemakers, a careful selection of instructors, and the employment of good teaching methods. In a recognition of these needs there is no proposal, however, to segregate those majoring in homemaking from other students who are not specializing in some one of the physical or social sciences. Since at least a majority of men and women marry, it seems reasonable to believe that the object of most college courses should be training for intelligent family life and citizenship. One cannot hazard an opinion regarding the members of a student body, either men or women, who will not marry, hence one cannot separate them into those who need training and those who will have no use for it. Naturally those who are looking forward to being chemical engineers or research economists would need more technical courses. In order that the student, man or woman, who enters upon family life may be well equipped to help in the conduct of the household and to secure the satisfactions which it holds, the entire four years must be used to the very best advantage and be built upon a knowledge of the needs of present-day families. *Conclusions.*—In this comparison of needs and trends, several observations and questions have been reserved until the detailed statements were made. Undoubtedly there has been, and still is, a focusing of attention upon the teaching of homemaking skills. Training for parenthood has but recently been added, and training for marriage has scarcely been attempted, partly, to be sure, because the needs are not yet clearly defined. Perhaps the following statements might be made: that the training of the past has been primarily in the techniques of homemaking, with emphasis upon good standards in the routine processes carried on in the home; that at the present time a transition from processes to persons, particularly the young child, is occurring; and that in the future one may anticipate more emphasis upon philosophy, perspective, personnel of the family, factors promoting successful marriage and family life, the use of leisure, and the rôle of home managers as citizens and community builders. Whereas college training in the past has been given largely to a group of women who have majored in home economics, frequently for a double reason—that of becoming economically independent and preparing for homemaking—the college training of the future will not be limited to special groups nor will it be provided so largely within a single department. If courses can be made valuable for men and women who are majoring in other fields, and if the prerequisites for such courses are few, the time is not far distant when one need no longer choose between education for marriage and parenthood and that for earning. In fact, one finds already in but nine institutions seven courses which have been planned primarily for students in departments other than home economics (*See* Table XV). If one were to include the courses in psychology, sociology, and economics in even a few institutions the number would be considerably larger.

One weakness which appears to exist in the present curricula, if one can judge by catalog material, is the separation of courses from present-day home life. Although the laboratory of the engineer is frequently the construction center, and that of the medical student is the hospital, the student of family life depends upon literature rather than upon observation and participation. The difficulties in providing home contacts and in keeping an objective point of view are recognized. If a coöperative plan interferes with relationships and goals, it is an undesirable one to encourage; yet there is a need for studying family life at close range and under varied conditions, if the student is to have a picture of it. This need is particularly urgent if the setting of the college, the living arrangements of the students, and the experience of the teaching faculty are such that the students are out of touch with actual families. Contacts with the homes and families of children in the nursery school, home management residence courses, home projects, and field work among families of limited means help to meet the need. In a few instances facilities of the extension service may also provide help. Naturally the associations of the individual in her own home and in those of relatives and close friends does provide a background, but one that is usually regarded less objectively.

The effect of the personal traits and attitudes of men

and women in promoting stable, satisfying, and successful family life[15] would seem to point to the need for more attention to the development of desirable qualities throughout college. Without exceedingly skillful guidance more harm than good can come of the best intended program. While many behaviorists may argue that the college period is years too late for any permanently beneficial results, the subject is one which is open to research and demonstration. In these days of huge student bodies and large classes in a more impersonal institution, the personality of the individual student is often the only phase of his being which escapes attention unless he is either "queer" or very popular.

Another aspect of family life which has received both tardy and scant recognition is the use of leisure. With the multiplicity of opportunities for employing the hours of free time and the reserve in energy, the difficulty of making satisfactory choices is very much greater. In a day when living is accompanied by many tensions, the ability to carry responsibilities calmly and to relax is partly a matter of having intriguing diversions that keep the individual fit. Training for marriage and parenthood is incomplete if it fails to provide an introduction to and the incentive for interests that are apart from the responsibilities associated with earning and managing the routine activities of the home. Men and women who are absorbed by their responsibilities are less likely to be comrades and coöperators in family and community life.

[15] Chase Going Woodhouse, in reporting on a study of "Successful Family Life," includes the following statement: "Outstandingly, then, the group felt that it was the attitudes, personal traits, and relationships between the members of the family which counted most in developing a successful family life. Of the total 2,208 essentials listed 1,136 fell under this head."—*Social Forces*, VIII, 516.

There are several examples of men and women among
these families who need diverting outlets if they are to
keep their perspective on life, and there are children who
are being deprived of fellowship in recreation by a lack
of outside interests on the part of one or both parents.
There is a tendency in several of the nine institutions studied to encourage the election of courses in departments
other than home economics. One institution lists a group
of "appreciation courses (music, drama, art, literature)"[16]
to the extent of four hours as a requirement for graduation from the liberal course in home economics. In addition practically one-third of this entire course is made up
of free electives. One wishes, however, that a part of
the electives permitted in many institutions might be taken
in the first two years of college rather than that the development of these leisure time interests should be postponed until the student is two years older.

The importance of physical fitness to the psychic, social, and economic aspects of family life has already been
stressed. In analyzing the curricula, attention to the
management of the health of the family seems to be
lacking. With the exception of the courses in personal
hygiene, there are but four institutions which make a
course in health a requirement. Only six would have
the student equipped with the background which physiology provides. Undoubtedly the training in nutrition
should be regarded as a part of disease prevention, but
even with the most intelligent management of food for
the family, courses in management which relate directly
to the other factors promoting health seem desirable. In
health, as in the various aspects of family life, there is

[16] *Bulletin of the University of Nebraska, College of Agriculture Announcements 1929-1930*, p. 39.

need for setting up the problems of adjustment which
· homemakers actually encounter and letting these become
the basis for selection of subject matter. Those problems
which appear to handicap development most seriously are
the ones on which to center attention from the angle of
methods of prevention.

In the preceding chapter mention has been made of
the fact that experience in family life makes certain issues much more clear-cut than they could have been in
the pre-marriage and pre-parental period, when responsibilities have not yet been carried. In view of this fact,
and with the knowledge that the task of a college administration is the education of its student body, the question of whether graduation should mark the close of the
institution's contribution to the student may well be
raised. To the writer it seems that the addition of facilities which will enable an alma mater to provide further
training for family life and further contacts to this end are
not only justified but highly important. The types of service provided by nursery schools for the education both
of parent and child is a step in this direction. In many
instances, extension divisions provide the unit of organization. There remains to be developed the type of counsel which can help men and women with the background
of a university education to promote a larger measure of
success and satisfaction in family life.

In concluding this presentation of college trends in
training for marriage and parenthood, the limitations of
the study need to be recalled, lest the observations appear to be more representative than the material justifies.
The nine institutions studied were chosen because they
furnished the college training for more than half of the
home economics women who were coöperators in the

present inquiry regarding home problems and family life. The findings are not based upon an analysis of all of the courses offered in each institution, but only upon those that were listed as a part of the general major in home economics. The objectives, the content of the courses now offered, and the present points of emphasis were determined by the titles and the descriptions given in the catalogs. Finally, this summary has dealt only with the needs of wives and mothers and with the facilities which are open at present, because of tradition and circumstances, to one sex rather than to both.

CHAPTER VIII

THE PLACE OF THE COMMUNITY IN PROMOTING SUCCESSFUL FAMILY LIFE

THE DEGREE to which families are dependent upon the communities in which they live is apparent at every turn. The number and type of resources affect the ease with which goals are neared, the time that is required, and the cost to the individual family. In the present study a wide variation is found in the extent to which a community serves its families.

If a locality were to be given a high rating on its ability to promote stable and satisfying family life, rather than solely on its industrial and commercial opportunities —a test that is more frequently applied—what institutions and agencies would be regarded as indispensable? Questions relating to the helps in family life that have been received from communities furnish information on this point.

Educational Agencies.—For families with children a good system of public schools is indispensable. Such a system includes not alone a course of study which is suited to the needs of the individual child from six to eighteen years of age, but good buildings, and a corps of instructors who know subject matter *and* human nature. There is a tendency on the part of this group of parents to want provision made for lengthening the period in school by adding kindergartens and colleges. Some who have had the advantage of a nursery school, and others who would like access to one, would have the help of qualified teachers begin in the years that are regarded by many as the pre-school period.

In an era which is coming to be characterized by its opportunity for leisure, the need for wise choice in determining the interests to which one devotes his free time seems important to parents. So education that prepares one for earning is but a part of the good curriculum. The school system which helps the child to be a more discriminating person and to acquire skill in whatever field for which his special abilities may fit him is of incalculable value to both parent and child. Public school music and many of the extra-curricular activities are examples of developments which parents regard with satisfaction unless the demands made upon the child are out of proportion to his strength and time.

In the matter of the development of moral and ethical standards the home looks to the school, for there is a realization that in the hours away from the parents the child needs to have a standard maintained that is in keeping with that which is set in the home. Too little thought or emphasis by local educators upon this phase of development creates confusion in the mind of boy and girl, and often a departure from the course which has been charted by the parents. The standards of the neighborhood also affect those which can be maintained within the family, thus serving as an educational influence either for good or ill.

To be within reach of a school system is one thing; to have it really accessible is another. For the rural family tuition charges in the city school, when there are several children to see through high school, may result in providing them with the poorer foundation of a one-room, or at most a two-room rural school. Difficulties in securing transportation, and the more costly alternative of paying for room and board in town, often result in accepting a second-best choice. For these families the consolidated school and the school bus have been a boon to child and adult, not only in affording better opportunities, but in affording them through a longer school year.

For the urban family the accessibility of the school is also important, particularly when the children are young. The speed and the amount of traffic on highways have greatly increased the need for attention to the location of buildings and to the use of devices for insuring safety on the way to and from school. Railroad crossings are today but one of several dangers which keep mothers anxious until the children have actually reached home.

Even though not all families coöperate as fully as they think they should, there is an appreciation of the need for parents to have an understanding of the objectives of the teachers, a knowledge of the methods which are used in the schoolroom, and personal contacts with the instructors. Since the school of the present day supplements the training of the home, in a larger number of fields than those of the three R's, knowledge of what each institution is attempting to accomplish, the methods it is using, and the problems which arise are essential for both parents and teachers. For very nearly one-third of the entire number in the group studied, the Parent-Teacher Association, or one which is similar in its purpose, helps to develop coöperative relationships. In several instances mothers feel that the organization is dominated too largely by the viewpoint of the teaching group and that there is a failure to grasp the perspective of the parent.

Classrooms and laboratories are not the only part of the educational plant which is desirable in a community. One out of three of the women in this study list a library

as an invaluable asset.[1] Many of those who live where they
have access to good collections of books and periodicals
find them indispensable for adults as well as for children,
and those who reside in more remote areas regret the lack
of such facilities. While home libraries are desired, the cost
to the individual family of a private collection providing
the most necessary books of reference which are usually
available through a library, frequently makes it prohibitive.

In connection with the provision for the educational
needs of the family, it is interesting to discover that a great
many of the families are living in towns and cities where
colleges and universities are located. While the selection
of the locality has resulted in many cases from the professional opportunities afforded for the man, there are
numerous instances in which the atmosphere of the college locality, in addition to the educational advantages
for the whole family, has seemed to outweigh the
economic sacrifices which have been necessary.

Thus far the choice of a community, in terms of the
educational facilities for the children in the family, has
been noted. But in this day of adult education many
husbands and wives are evaluating communities also in
terms of the facilities which there are for continuing their
own education. For the husband a less remunerative position, if the work and the environment permit the completion of an advanced degree or other satisfactions of a
non-economic nature, frequently becomes the more desirable one. Among the college trained women partic-

[1] According to a study made in 1926 by the American Library Association,
the following facilities were available at that time: 44 per cent of the total
population of the U. S. are without access to local public libraries. 6 per
cent of the entire urban population are without public library service, and 83
per cent of the entire rural population are without such service.

ularly there is a tendency to show a marked preference for communities in which they will have educational opportunities and contacts. For some of the graduates who live in rural districts the lack of stimulating associations is felt keenly. Where there are Home Bureaus, a local League of Women Voters, or study clubs devoted to any one of a number of interests the remoteness from colleges and urban centers is less of a handicap. The importance of an environment which is mentally stimulating to the wife is likely to be recognized to an increasing degree as more of the women who marry have had the opportunities provided by college training and associations.

Religious Institutions.—There appears to be an appreciation by these parents that a community with churches and their related activities makes the conduct of family life more inspirational and successful. Slightly more than five out of every ten families go to services each week; four out of ten attend occasionally; and only twelve families out of the entire group—four in each one hundred— —state that they do not go to church at all. The weekly church school and women's auxiliaries are both regarded as important phases of the religious life of the family and an effort is made to support them.

There is a dependence upon the paid and the lay leaders of the church for instruction of the children in religion. Whether this is due to a lack of information on the part of the parents, an inability to interpret their own beliefs in language which the child can understand, a lack of time in an age of new leisure, or a feeling of insecurity regarding the faith which is within them, is not clear. In this respect the demand of the family upon the community is different from that which was made in a day when family worship and other religious traditions were a part of the daily routine in every home. Even as the school has absorbed a larger part of the responsibility for secular education, so these families are relying upon the church to provide the religious education for the child.

The essentials to be provided by the religious institutions are less clear from the comments of the mothers than are their requirements of the educational institutions. Some find in the weekly services which they attend the inspiration that is needed for carrying cheerfully their daily responsibilities. Others get from the sermons educational stimulation and a broader outlook on present-day issues, the extent depending, however, upon the ability and the background of the minister, and the degree to which they accept his analyses of current problems. Without question the church is for many, particularly those living in the smaller cities and rural districts, a social center which promotes friendships and a recognition of common interests.

While there are divisions within the church on the basis of sex and age, a part of its program is designed for the whole family. Those activities are among the few that are conducted outside the home today which promote a unity of interests and associations. Both within and between families the church appears to provide an integrating influence.

Social and Recreational Institutions.—In the matter of social and recreational institutions communities may be either too active or too indifferent in providing opportunities for the family. The city is not always an example of an over-active community, nor do the rural district and town prove to be the localities in which too little provision is made. On the contrary, there are frequent references to the multiplicity of demands that are made upon the leisure and semi-leisure hours of the individual members in the small city and village. That these demands interfere with the time that the family has for group pleasures is apparent; that it is difficult, also, for the members to know how and when to say no is brought out by many of the women.

Aside from the wide range in the extent of the opportunities and demands in different communities, there is a variation in the amount available for the members at different ages. While one rural woman has unlimited calls to take part in professional and social programs, her adolescent son is without close associations or interests since he has left school. In one neighborhood both parents have numerous social obligations, but an only child without outside interests and contacts with other children is a product of a grown-up world. Numerous comments illustrate similar unbalanced programs.

Among the lacks which appear most frequently in the social and recreational setting of the family is the absence of groups of parents with standards for their children that are similar to those of the woman reporting. Policies or conduct that are widely different from what the mother desires create friction between parents and children and anxiety regarding the child's development. Where there are parents' organizations in which community standards and the best methods of attaining them become the central topic for discussion, coöperative projects can be developed to advantage. The difficulty of keeping up with the Jones's, which seems more important to the adolescent son or daughter than to other members of the family, is reduced if there is agreement of the parents and if their backgrounds are similar.

Parks, play space for children, and supervised playgrounds constitute another lack that is observed by very nearly one in five mothers. Without having these recreational facilities easily accessible the degree of supervision and the constancy of the demands made upon the mothers are very much greater. Particularly is this true during the summer vacation when there are the free school hours in addition to the play hours of the other nine months. Those who have access to boys' and girls' clubs, Y. M. C. A. buildings, gymnasiums, tennis courts, swimming pools, and play space regard them as very great helps.

Agencies for Promoting Health.—In the matter of health the degree of help received from the community determines in large measure the money, the time, and the strength that remain for other things. An adequate program of public health is as indispensable as one of public education, and a lack of it may prove even more costly to the community. When there is a lack of attention to sanitation, to the prevention of epidemics, and to the control of infectious diseases by public officials, family members are less fit physically than they might well expect to be. In one small village, a policy of allowing children's diseases to be spread, on the theory that each child must have them at some time before he becomes an adult, has interfered seriously with the degree of freedom from illness in one home where three children had both whooping cough and chicken pox in a single winter, not to mention innumerable colds. In this respect the more careful inspection and frequent quarantines in cities make them a safer place for keeping children well than are many small towns where less responsibility is felt.

Clinics for mothers and infants for general diagnostic services, for dental services, and for the treatment of specific diseases, such as tuberculosis, often shorten the period of illness and cut down the number of fatalities, provided they are available to the moderate income group —the group which is frequently unable to pay for the services of specialists out of the margin that is left beyond routine needs during health. When hospitals and nurses are also available at a cost that is not excessive for this group, the strain of illness is greatly lessened. In the degree to which the savings of the years can be depleted by the costs of illness, only the orgy of a stock market collapse presents a comparison.

Public Utilities and Services.—The amounts of time, energy, and money that are required to keep the family comfortable depend upon the number and the cost of the public utilities which are available. The mother in the rural home that is without modern conveniences has three choices: more hours used daily in doing routine tasks, acceptance of a standard for housekeeping and group associations that is below the one which she regards as desirable, or a larger amount of help from members of the family and paid service. Among the helps from the community which women mention frequently are telephones, electricity, gas, a city water supply and sewerage system, garbage disposal, and good transportation. For those living in industrial centers ordinances which actually lessen the nuisance of smoke decrease the cost of keeping the house and the family clean. If there is adequate provision for the care of streets and walks, the amount of dirt that enters through the openings and is carried into the house is greatly reduced.

As might be expected, there is a wide variation in the marketing facilities provided in towns and cities. This affects the degree of choice, the time required for serving as the family's purchasing agent, and the proportion of the income that is needed for each item of the budget. If one lives in a city where farmers' markets are encouraged by officials, the costs of fruits, vegetables, eggs, and poultry are lower. When cash-and-carry groceries, cut-rate drug stores, and dependable department stores, which sell at reasonable prices, are accessible the cost of living can be appreciably decreased. The opportunity to choose ready-to-wear garments at a price that is within the allotment provided for clothing helps to shorten the working day of the mother and to decrease the nervous strain upon her.

When there are commercial agencies which perform in a satisfactory manner and at a reasonable cost services previously done by members of the family, housekeeping can become less than a full-time occupation. While 22 per cent of the families studied use the services of a commercial laundry, or a hand laundress who takes the family wash to her home, there are many who find that the problem of laundering is not satisfactorily handled. Either the weekly cost of the service seems disproportionate, or the wear and tear on the linens and clothing makes the replacement cost exceedingly high. Among the needs of these families, both urban and rural, there is probably none that is greater than a satisfactory plan which would encourage them to send both washing and ironing out of the home. One wonders why provision for this need might not be developed like any other public utility, with able scientists directing the technical procedure, to the end that fabrics would be kept intact, with sanitation in the process insured.

Another need of the family for which provision is frequently lacking in the community is a supply of skilled or semi-skilled employees for household tasks. Even with the transfer of a part of these tasks to outside agencies, the constancy of the demands upon mothers makes many women less fit for the responsibilities of family life than they would be if they could rely upon assistants to relieve them from a part of the routine work. For many mothers the direction of several active children with widely different personalities is most difficult because of the multiplicity of tasks which cannot be postponed, such, for example, as the three meals a day, the washing and the ironing, the cleaning, and the mending. The family income limits the amount of service which can be afforded, yet part-time help could often be managed if there were skilled persons available to give such assistance. The matter of household employees deserves the attention of communities that desire to promote successful family life.

In a day when there is an increased appreciation of what the first six years of life mean to the individual, the policy of allowing children to be surrounded by unwholesome influences because of economic considerations seems in reality a costly, although not always a conscious, one. There have been frequent references to the fatigue and worry that accompany the constant responsibility for younger members of one's family and the extent to which this falls upon the mother, partly because she is likely to be the one adult that remains at home. As has been pointed out in the preceding paragraph, if this were the *only* responsibility carried during the hours the strain would be lessened. For some women the chance to turn routine tasks over to a paid helper or other members of the family, thus giving more freedom to direct the children, provides a satisfactory solution; for others who are less skillful with children and those who have less insight or interest in child nature, there is the need for persons or agencies to which the family may look for some release for the mother.

Aside from a few communities in which nursery schools are provided through the college or university, there is no record of a community which accepts the care of young children as a part of its responsibility. In one neighborhood a plan of exchange was worked out by a group of mothers and it has been exceedingly helpful in freeing several women from the supervision of young children for five out of six mornings of each week. The plan is one in which each of the mothers accepts the responsibility for her own and her neighbors' children through one morning weekly. In a few instances the lack of provision for children after they graduate from nursery school, but before they are old enough to enter the kindergarten or first grade, is indicated as a handicap. *Occupational Opportunities for Married Women.*—An opportunity for continuing in a remunerative occupation is desired by many in this group of women, which is composed largely of college graduates and in which there are several who hold advanced degrees. In some communities, principally the urban ones, there are openings which permit wives and mothers to pursue careers for which their training fits them; in the smaller cities and rural areas, where there are few opportunities, several have turned to other lines of work which required less technical training because such work helped to increase the income or furnish outside interests. The underlying reason for wishing to continue with earning, or return to it, is not always clear, nor is there any one explanation which seems to apply equally in all cases; but the fact that ten women were carrying full-time positions in addition to homemaking at the time they replied to the questionnaire, and that forty-four—15 per cent—reported part-time work, is significant. Besides the 18 per cent employed there were others who deplored their inability to find "something to do," and some who looked forward to going on with their work when the children were older or present conditions were altered.

For communities desiring to promote successful family life this issue is a very pertinent one. The question is no longer one which can be lightly dismissed. "It isn't done" or "It shouldn't be done" are two glibly used phrases that are not easily justified in an era when comparisons with an earlier generation show so many contrasts. With the increasing number of trained women who are entering marriage and parenthood by way of a career and economic independence, the conditions are different. This conviction that circumstances alter conditions is expressed by very nearly three out of four of the husbands who furnished information on the advisability of having their wives work at an occupation in addition to that of homemaking. Less than three out of each ten were unwilling for their wives to be employed for pay.

Until the conclusions from several comprehensive studies of families on different educational, economic, and social levels are made available, there is no way of knowing the effects of the employment of wives and mothers upon the women themselves, their relationships with their husbands, the number of children born and reared, the degree to which the children are helped or handicapped, family stability and satisfactions, and the employment of others, both men and unmarried women. The present lack of information makes the formulation of community policies difficult and at best but tentative. *Extent of Participation in Enterprises of the Community.* —Though the home is dependent upon the institutions and agencies of the community, the number and the type which are developed in any locality grow out of the activities which the families of the communities initiate and support. In this connection the amount of leadership and of coöperation furnished by a selected group of families, with educational advantages for the parents far above the average of a cross-section of the population, is interesting. Information regarding the part taken by the women is greater than for other members of the families.

In the entire group of women, outside interests which had been uppermost before marriage have been retained by approximately seven out of ten. Slightly less than two in ten found it necessary to alter or drop the contacts beyond the home. Many indicated that there was difficulty in meeting appointments away from home while the children are young. For the group of home economics graduates, only six in ten reported a continuation of the extra-household activities, and three in ten indicated lessened activities or a withdrawal from them. If the family had lived in several localities for short periods of time, the members seemed less likely to enter into activities in the communities.

The support of school and church was found among six out of every ten of the women who listed active interest in each of these two institutions. For the home economics graduates, a slightly smaller percentage of women indicated attendance at church or help with its related activities. Only four in ten showed an active interest in the school system, but many added that only until their children were old enough to be enrolled were they limiting their contacts.   One half of the entire group of those who indicate active support are members of Parent-Teacher Associations, and a similar proportion visits the sessions.   Smaller numbers entertain the teachers, serve on committees, or accept membership on Boards of Education.   Conferences with the teachers, voting at school elections, assisting with social functions, teaching, initiating desirable changes, and acting as advisers were further expressions of interest by some.

Memberships in clubs primarily for diversion were held by as large a proportion of the entire group as that active in church and school, but among the home economics group the ratio fell from six in ten to three in ten. Activity in college organizations, however, among the latter group was found somewhat more often.   Interest in study clubs and organizations designed to make women more skillful in the conduct of households and the development of children was reported by slightly more than a quarter of the entire group; for the home economics group the ratio is slightly less than one in ten.

One in five of all the women takes an active part in civic movements; for the home economics women the ratio is but slightly lower.   In addition to the interests that have been reported, many refer to membership in a woman's club, which may be either literary or civic in purpose, in musical clubs, and in professional organizations.   Contacts with business associates of the husbands are maintained by many.

Conclusions.—From the foregoing summary of needs and interests one gathers that the degree to which the community, the state, and the nation serve the family is dependent in part upon the demands which groups of families make and the policies they adopt. Clearly defined goals and techniques are important in obtaining results, but continuing collective action is essential in building an environment that promotes physical, mental, and social fitness. An investment of energy, time, and money in affairs of the community is likely to pay both tangible and intangible dividends which directly benefit the family.

CHAPTER IX

THE PROMOTION OF HEALTHFUL AND
SATISFYING FAMILY LIFE—
A SUMMARY

HEALTHFUL FAMILY LIFE, as it is used here, means a
home environment in which each individual member of
the group is enabled to reach his greatest stature physically, mentally, emotionally, and socially without loss
of time or talents in the process. In other words, the development is a continuously ascending process. Further,
healthful family life implies that the group is able not
only to carry its own weight in the larger units of which
it is a part, but also to enable these larger groups to function more successfully. Satisfying family life means
that the home environment provides for the desires of
each individual, in so far as these desires are consistent
with the promotion of physical and social fitness, to such a
degree that happiness and contentment result for the several members of the group.

In earlier chapters there has been considerable emphasis placed upon the need for an adequate income
which can be earned under conditions that do not im-
pair the health or the comradeship of the members of
the group. The greater dependence of present-day families upon money incomes makes adequacy the more important. The weakened bargaining power of the individual creates a series of new problems in choice and economy. The larger number of demands upon the income
by the younger members of the family creates additional
problems. One finds also that adequacy is not a term
which can be defined satisfactorily by means of a simple
set of figures.

[157]

The multiplicity of the demands upon wives and mothers continues in the twentieth century, though the nature of these new demands varies from those made upon an earlier generation of homemakers. To meet the responsibilities of family life and to increase the satisfactions derived from it, education for marriage and parenthood is wholly desirable. Thus far attention seems to have been centered upon technical aspects of homemaking, and courses have been provided largely for women either before or after marriage. Educational opportunities have not been limited to curricula of the classroom, but, particularly in recent years, local and national organizations have fostered study groups, demonstration centers, and, in a few instances nursery schools and kindergartens accompanied by a program of parental, as well as of child, education. A flood of literature dealing with the various aspects of homemaking, particularly the development of children, is now available, and this is more or less useful depending, in part, upon the experiences, the insight, and the appreciation of the authors. The need for education that is constructive in its approach and practical in its viewpoint is seen from the comments of mothers.

An increasing leisure and the recognition that comradeship is an exceedingly important phase of family life makes attention to the means of securing leisure and of using it with satisfaction both to the individual and to the group, a need to be recognized by educators and by leaders in other fields. With education for earning provided for women as well as for men, and with increasing vocational opportunities available for women, the values in marriage and family life may well be brought out. More attention, too, to methods whereby life may be successfully directed, at the same time that a position with a salary is held, is in line with modern conditions.

The present study has furnished no information regarding the types of education that are available and useful for men who become husbands and fathers. The need for administrators to appreciate that there are two to get ready for marriage and parenthood, as Ernest R. Groves has said, is apparent from the comments of both the wives and husbands. Differences in attitudes, appreciations, and standards, particularly in the development of children, are the more noticeable and upsetting in family life when the education received by women has put them in touch with recent scientific facts regarding health and human nature. While the personal traits and the intelligence of both men and women may lessen the amount of discontent and friction that result from these differences, there is a strong likelihood that so long as the major portion of the training given the members of one sex is limited to that received in the homes of their childhood, unified goals and methods will be found less frequently in family life. Arguments of husband and wife regarding the cost of food, the type of house needed for the group, the diet of the child, and many other matters can be traced directly to two very different educational routes. As a condition, therefore, for the promotion of healthful and satisfying family life, the training of boys and of men is not less important than that of girls and women. To center attention upon one sex is educating but half of the parents, and this policy may actually lead to less rather than more harmonious relationships.

Mary Hinman Abel in her book, *Successful Family Life on a Moderate Income,* has listed generous help on the part of the community as one of the four conditions necessary to insure successful family life. The comments of the men and women in the present study have emphasized the extent to which a home must rely upon the community, not alone for economic opportunity in earning, but for coöperation in maintaining desired standards and for the provision of various institutions and agencies to supplement the goods and services of the individual family. There are innumerable forces outside of the home which are only in part—and in some cases but slightly, if at all—under the control of the heads of families. Such forces can either complicate or simplify the conduct of family life. The increased mobility found under modern conditions makes contacts, close friendships, and interests more difficult to maintain, and thus a new type of family isolation, one which exists in the midst of crowds, tends to appear.

Soundness of body and of mind constitutes one of the most important conditions for the promotion of health and satisfaction among the members of the group. The degree of health and the period over which it extends affect the perspective, as well as the accomplishments, of the members. Preventive measures pay large dividends in terms of well being and financial savings. The services of expert diagnosticians, practitioners, surgeons, dentists, and other specialists represent investments which increase the probability of early and complete recovery. Chronic or acute ailments and disease may handicap the family in countless ways. A lack of strength or vitality often diminishes the earning power or depletes the income with amazing rapidity. It limits the zest with which the easily fatigued person enters into plans for recreation and the degree of inspiration and refreshment he secures from outside interests. Relationships within and outside the group are likely to be less satisfactory, for the person who is below par may be exceedingly sensitive, or selfish and self-centered. Because of his demands, or because of the desire of other members to minister to his every want, the environment becomes a much less normal or desirable setting for those who remain well.

The philosophy of parents and the developing attitudes of children exert a profound influence on the individuals in the group and upon the satisfactions which are possible. It is here that one sees the effect of the early home training and the supplementary background of later experiences which the heads of families have had. There are numerous tributes paid by the women to their parents, or to others of mature years, for an expression, an attitude, or a goal that has made life more meaningful and the associations, in such an intimate group as the family, less trying than they would have been without it. Where philosophies are of the type that create serenity of mind, steadfastness of purpose, an appreciation of the potentialities of widely different personalities, and a joy in living, one of the greatest helps to health and satisfaction of the entire group is present.

The place of goals, both immediate and remote, in promoting healthful and satisfying family life is a point upon which there are lengthy comments. When all are looking forward to something with pleasure, the necessary routine and the sacrifices seem less irritating. Budgets of money, schedules of time, and a just division of labor and responsibilities are devices which make the nearing of goals more certain and more rapid. There is likely to be less bickering, less argument, and more willing coöperation, provided all who are able have had a share in formulating the goals toward which each will strive. The practice of including children in the discussions of the family and of increasing, as they grow older, the part which they take, brings desirable results. In homes where there are relatives or paid workers, recognition of their ideas and interests promotes frankness, understanding, and harmony. In the case of paid helpers the rate of turnover is greatly reduced.

Traditions often have a very useful place in promoting satisfactions. In a sense they may be regarded as expressions of goals, either in whole or in part. If they are in keeping with the needs of the family, rather than mere customs which have been passed down and observed only because of the past, and with much of the earlier meaning gone, they become an added force in the maintenance of interest and affections. Among the families in this study there are various traditions about which the attention of the entire group centers. The special festivities that are a part of every Christmas "since the first baby came," the observance of Thanksgiving in a particular way, the baskets at Easter for the neighbors, the hanging of wreaths, the birthday surprises, the annual family reunion—these are but a few of the traditions that are something more than mere customs for both adults and children. Because they frequently include relatives and old friends and because they often center about a place, a room, or a much loved vacation spot, the modern touch-and-go system of living makes the reproduction of well-remembered scenes and occasions the more difficult, though not impossible. When the preparations for these special occasions, or the actual participation in them, becomes either too strenuous or too costly, the advantages of continuing them indefinitely without simplifying them may be outweighed by the disadvantages.

"A place for everything and everything in its place," is an adage expressing a need which continues to be felt. When the housing is designed and equipment is selected to provide adequately for the various processes in the home and the activities of the group, work is greatly simplified, hours of housekeeping, dressing, and undressing are shortened, and clearly defined sources of irritation, fatigue, and friction are reduced. Each member of the family, even though he is young, is able to help himself much more than he can when suitable space for his possessions and activities is lacking. In an era of home rentals, rather than of home ownership, the family has less freedom in making alterations and additions; hence selection becomes even more important. Frequently fad and fashion in both housing and equipment, even as in matters of food and clothing, complicate the activities and increase the time required for them. In addition, they necessitate larger expenditures of money. An answer to the question of what constitutes a desirable minimum in housing and equipment for the health, convenience, comfort, and æsthetic appreciations of modern families would be exceedingly helpful in indicating essentials from the viewpoint of the consumer, in contrast with those which are set up by developers of real estate and dealers in furniture and equipment. Recommendations of electric washers and other expensive equipment for the individual home are not often based upon an unbiased comparison of all possible methods for solving the problem of laundry, but upon the articles which are on the market and the profits which dealers hope to make. In brief, the location of the home, the nature of the dwelling, the grounds, and the equipment affect the standards which can be maintained and the possibilities of growth.

The ability to direct the use of the human and material resources of the home and the family toward goals that have been defined affects the degree of health and satisfaction which can be achieved. The formulation of policies and goals is but a first step, a preliminary, to management. Ordering the activities of the home in accordance with the policies and the plans that have been formulated is the important and difficult part. Despite the amount of routine which family life involves, there are also many emergencies which arise. Adaptability thus becomes a cardinal asset for successful directors of families. For some people interruptions are nothing less than calamities; for others they constitute welcome diversions that can usually be fitted into a plan that is provided with marginal minutes. When these interruptions become too numerous or too lengthy, a revised plan provides a solution that saves one's disposition and prevents fatigue. Those who find the greatest satisfaction in family life appear to be those who see in management a method of making goals more nearly attainable. It is but a tool which they enjoy using because it brings results.

Plans by which a family can live involve an intelligent consideration of all the resources and the needs of the group. The wise mother anticipates the situations which are likely to arise from too little sleep, too much excitement, or constipation, and provides in the plan for the physical needs of the child. In the coöperative home these needs are also recognized by the father and he assists in living by schedule. The satisfactory financial plan is based upon the certain receipts in dollars and cents together with the needs. Definite information regarding past assets and liabilities increases the ease and the satisfaction with which new budgets are made.

The process of altering and perfecting plans is an essential one because wide fluctuations occur both in the resources and in the needs of a given group. These variations are partly the result of growing up. To use an obvious example, the schedule for meal hours is not the same for the very young and the older children, nor are the hours for sleep the same when the child once of preschool years reaches the age to enter high school. So, too, the financial needs are entirely different during the year that a new baby arrives, the family moves, or a son goes to college from what they are when these situations do not occur. Changes in income or in occupation may either necessitate or permit certain shifts in practices which would not otherwise be desirable.

Both men and women may be vastly more successful in the management of activities that concern only themselves than they are in those which involve others. Management of technical processes is less difficult than the direction of persons. From those who appear to be good personnel managers there are several suggestions for the promotion of satisfying family life. The practice of delegating responsibility in proportion to one's ability to assume it encourages willing participation and development. Working with the inexperienced person until techniques are developed and standards which are reasonable to expect of the assistant are clearly demonstrated increases the degree of skill, harmony, and satisfaction. Increasing the share of the learner from one lesson to another is the mark of the successful teacher who is present primarily to direct and not to do the task.

The division of responsibility which works best in the home is that which is based upon the interests, abilities, and free time of members of the group. While the major share of the physical care of the children must frequently rest upon the mothers, there are certain phases of the child's education which fathers may be able to provide more satisfactorily. In one home an explanation of death was one which a mother felt herself to be wholly unfitted to give; in many homes the giving of information to boys regarding matters of sex is delegated to the father. There is a question whether the hard and fast division of labor that is based upon sex is a desirable one to continue on the assumption of difference in fitness. For example, the tendency to exempt boys from household tasks even in their earliest years cannot but complicate their attitudes toward their responsibilities if they become husbands and fathers.

Consistency and fairness in the treatment accorded each member reduces the amount of misunderstanding and friction. The effect of abiding by clearly formulated policies which are understood by all concerned is seen in resulting attitudes. Reasonableness in dealing with requests and time for furnishing explanations when they are needed promote confidence in the motive and the judgment of the person who makes the decision. In addition, this procedure results in the good will of the person accepting the decision. A policy of fair play in matters of demands made and time required, of hours away from work, and extra pay for overtime decreases the rate of turnover with paid assistance. Expressed appreciation often makes the difference between encouragement and discouragement, between willingness and unwillingness.

The plan of "taking turns" when there is a wide range in ages and interests, helps to build up an esprit de corps in the family and gives all members an opportunity to do the things they most enjoy. A diversity of interests is noted in most families, but the ability to unify them exists far less often. Where there is a willingness on the part of the parents to enter into the activities which give pleasure to the children and to do the things which the other parent wishes to do, the attitudes of the children are more likely to be coöperative. In some homes there is an attempt to cultivate the hobbies of other members of the family, with a considerable degree of unity and comradeship resulting. This is seen particularly in church attendance, in membership in clubs, and in various forms of outdoor life. In contrast with these homes, there are a few examples of families in which a spirit of contrariness prevails between two or more members.

Provision for some time for each member of the family to be away from the group encourages appreciations of the other members and reduces the causes of irritation. The intimacy of home ties taxes the finest and fairest individual, and it tends to enlarge his weaknesses as with a magnifying glass. Privacy in the home, outside diversions with other groups, and vacations from the family all help to keep one from overlooking the admirable traits of character that each person possesses and from expecting the impossible of one's family.

In the discussion of the management of group relationships, the part that personal traits of the directors play in the promotion of healthful and satisfying family life has been implied. The recognition by the parents that the education of children in social behavior and in the development of character is their most important task is indicative, too, of the difference which the possession of desirable traits of personality makes in the conduct of the household. Affection, consideration, open-mindedness, honesty, unselfishness, loyalty, tolerance, cooperation, and willingness to admit error—these are some of the traits which appear to promote harmony within the group and friendships with those outside the family.

The lower the income and the more numerous the demands that are made upon it, the greater is the need for the members of the group to be skillful in the actual processes of the home. If the standards of one member or of several are considerably higher than those which are attained in daily living, anxiety, discontent, and friction are much more likely to occur. For example, the preparation of food which is noticeably unpalatable, particularly when compared with that prepared by one's mother, decreases markedly the satisfaction which home provides for the husband whose wife is uninterested and inexperienced in the culinary art. The activities which one carries on poorly or those which one dislikes produce both fatigue and unhappiness. If there is a margin in the income which can be used for paid service in the home, or to buy the services and the products of commercial agencies, these dislikes and inabilities matter less. Obviously the domestic traits and abilities of the wives are of more importance than those of other members. However, the skill of the husband and his willingness to assist with the tasks of the household—as, for example, the making of necessary repairs, the care of the devices for heating, and the care of the grounds—do affect harmony and satisfactions. The ability which has been developed in even the youngest child lessens the strain upon the mother and the length of her day. It affects also the relationships that exist.

Changed and changing conditions of the present day make evaluations and the charting of courses for the family more difficult than is the process of carrying on according to unchanged and widely accepted standards. Throughout the comments of the men and women who have coöperated in this study, there are suggestions of the degree to which studies of the home and of family life can help them to gain a perspective on their undertaking and to analyze the situations which occur. The following chapter deals with research in the field of marriage and the family.

CHAPTER X

RESEARCH IN THE FIELD OF MARRIAGE AND THE FAMILY[1]

OBSTACLES in Conducting Scientific Studies.—In the present era there is an increased emphasis upon factual and inductive studies in all of the social sciences; as a consequence, there arises the question of approaches, methods, and specific procedures which can be used satisfactorily for scientific studies of the family. The universality of this institution limits the amount of reliable knowledge that can be secured. The very closeness to family life of practically every investigator and his domination, often unconsciously, by group mores and personal experiences make manifold the difficulties of conducting research. As in other studies of social phenomena, and more particularly in the case of the family, the elements and processes cannot be subjected either readily or easily to the critical analyses that are possible for the student in a chemical laboratory who is endeavoring to discover the physical and chemical properties of a new compound.

The student of the family is handicapped not only by the complexity of the unit and by his relation to it, but also by the dearth of tools for observation and measurement. The microscope and many of the other tools of the physical scientist do not serve him nor can they be adapted to his needs. The statistical method of both the physical and the social scientist may be employed satisfactorily for some studies, such as the *extent* of stability in marriage, yet prove inadequate in others as, for example,

[1] I wish to acknowledge my indebtedness to Howard W. Odum and Katharine Jocher for the help which I have received from them in writing this chapter.

[170]

the composite and interrelationship of factors promoting stability.[2]   The historical method is useful in presenting what has been, but direction and control of a changing economic order, to the end that human beings may live most happily and helpfully here and now, require in addition descriptions of the present situation.

To Odum and Jocher[3] there are two major problems to be recognized by all social scientists. The first is that of evolving and perfecting adequate methods, and the second is that of mastering the human elements involved in both the search for social truth and in its extension to the social realm. The difficulties which grow out of a mastery of the human factors appear to them to be the greater of the two and include "the prejudice of the investigator, on the one hand, and of those who give information and those who receive and interpret the results of social research, on the other. On the part of the investigator his results are conditioned by his prejudices or limitations in finding out the truth, in interpreting it, and in presenting the final results. The investigator may find what he is looking for only, or partially; he may classify his results according to preconceived arrangement, he may interpret them according to his wishes, and may present his findings, even if unknowingly, as rationalized products."[4]

The quantity of factual data regarding social phenomena that can be discovered is dependent upon the type of social analysis which is made by those conducting research. To quote Odum and Jocher again, "this involves . . . a successful procedure through which social phenom-

[2] See "Methods of Research in Studying the Family," by Katharine Jocher, in The Family; IX, 80-86.

[3] An Introduction to Social Research, p. 20.

[4] Ibid., pp. 316-18.

ena may be studied in such quantitative and particularistic fashion and so analyzed and interpreted as to reduce them to a *social denominator* or to social constants, as a basis for really scientific conclusions and synthesis. . . . The fallacy of forming fundamental judgments upon superficial variables or of attempting synthetic conclusions based upon unlike units assumed to be like is perhaps the most common defect of the old comparative method of social study."[5]   The very complexity of the data with which the social scientist is confronted makes the task of finding common denominators the more perplexing and is likely to promote all manner of false and hasty deduction.

A tendency to look for a cause-effect relationship, to reduce family life to a few simple formulæ, or to generalize from insufficient data is frequently found in studies of marriage and the family.   The need for limiting the field of inquiry by taking a small group to study, by focusing attention upon a few aspects of family life, or by carrying the study over a relatively short period of weeks or months, affects further the conclusions that may be drawn.   The wide variation in the extant types of homes and in the nature of the forces that affect them makes a representative sample more difficult to secure. Studies of selected homes and of certain aspects of family life may entirely conceal basic interrelationships.

Limitations of the Present Study of Needs of Families.— The findings in the study of 306 homes which have been reported in these chapters are not free from the shortcomings that have been suggested above.   As has been pointed out in Chapter II, there was no attempt made to secure the coöperation of a representative sample of American parents in answering the questionnaires.   Instead, the

[5] *Ibid.,* pp. 407-9.

selection was made deliberately on the basis of certain educational advantages which women had had. Whether their situations, attitudes, and practices are typical of all families with similar backgrounds cannot be answered until the results of other studies are available.

In addition to the need for checking on the accuracy of the present findings by making other studies of similar groups, there is also the importance of securing factual material regarding family life which is conducted on widely differing economic, educational, and social levels. There is an appreciation, too, of the difficulties which arise in attempting to gather data from men and women who may be either unable or unwilling to analyze their home situations and group relationships to the degree that those coöperating in the study reported here have done. With an apparently increasing number of childless homes, studies need to be made of the organization, goals, and relationships of this type of home as well as of those in which there are children. In studies that have been undertaken up to the present time, attention has been centered largely upon the home that has failed conspicuously. There is need for more studies of "successful" homes if the body of factual material is to be fully descriptive.

In brief, there will be adequate and reliable factual data regarding American marriage and the family only when unbiased studies of representative samples have been secured and when continuing supplementary investigations are conducted to give a picture of both the kaleidoscopic and the unchanging aspects of this institution. In another portion of the present chapter a more detailed statement is made regarding the nature of the data which need to be made available.

Reference has been made to the use of the question-

naire in the study which has been reported.⁶ The disadvantages of this technique are apparent. It is entirely possible that many of the attitudes may be intentionally and
skillfully, or unknowingly, concealed by the person furnishing information. Comments of the informants readily lend themselves to faulty interpretation when read
by a stranger apart from the actual setting of the family.
The comments which they make on one day and in one
mood may be different from those made on the same point
at another time. These difficulties are partly avoided
when questions that can be answered by yes or no, or
good checking lists, or a combination of the two, make
up the entire questionnaire. From the standpoint of the
ease and the accuracy with which a statistical report can
be prepared, such a questionnaire is preferable. However, much of the information which one often desires
to secure from families cannot be had as concisely as this
and, if one limits the informant to the one word answers
or checks, many of the most significant facts and attitudes
may be missed entirely.⁷ For some studies the briefer re-

⁶ See Appendix for the three forms used and the descriptive material introducing the study.

⁷ "No statistical study—aside from counting the number of apparently successful marriages and happy families in a given area—of the normal family
can ever be made that will be of any material value. There is no family, no
matter how well it is adjusted, that does not have problems to solve. No
two families have exactly the same problems nor can any two families solve
a similar problem exactly alike. All depends upon the constituent parts of
the family, the individual members who compose it. Therefore, to tabulate
problems and solutions and to work out correlations and percentages would
be of little direct value. But as in law, cases involving similar legal technicalities are cited to assist in making a decision with reference to the case on
trial and, in medicine, previous cases with similar symptoms often assist the
physician or surgeon in his diagnosis of a present patient, so studies of satisfactory family adjustments ought to prove invaluable in pointing the way
for others."—Katharine Jocher, "Methods of Research in Studying the Family,"
The Family, IX, 85.

ply will be sufficient; perhaps with increased skill in formulating projects a part of the labor involved for both the person replying and the compiler of the data can be greatly reduced.

In contrast with the use of a questionnaire, there is the interview either with or without a detailed schedule. In spite of the greater cost in terms of the expense that may be required for travel and the time of all who are interviewed, of the ease of digression—which may reveal some very significant points for the study—and of the personal equation, this technique is one which can well be tested in studies of family life more extensively than it has thus far been tested.

There is always the strong possibility that the results of research, in which either the questionnaire or the interview technique has been used, will either overemphasize or fail to stress the significant factors in a situation. Most homemakers are inarticulate in expressing the needs which arise in the conduct of their households. This is particularly true of their relationships with other members of the group. While the habit of deploring the high cost of living is widespread, as are other instances of economic need which many believe that a readjustment of the economic order could remedy, the rank and file are slow to analyze and interpret the weaknesses and strengths in their own experience. To be sure the new bride is likely to discuss her lack of culinary ability or the mother who is bringing up an only child is glad of an outlet for her pent-up emotions, but these are cases in which certain skills are clearly undeveloped and in which comparisons of results with those of other women are easily made. The reasons for a hesitation or refusal to provide a stranger with attitudes and happenings that touch the most intimate aspects of life are several. The ideals which many men and women hold for marriage and family life may make discussions with an "outsider" and supplying answers to their questions seem disloyal to one's family. When there is a lack of appreciation or of knowledge on the part of the questioner in the interview, or by one who is seeking to gather facts by means of a questionnaire, all approaches are discouraged. In other cases an unwillingness to see the situation from all angles and to recognize the disagreeable factors may limit expression. An inability to analyze situations and results, indifference, or satisfaction with conditions as they are is often responsible for the small amount of useful information secured.

In the present study the desire to secure information primarily regarding the relation of management to child development should be considered in an evaluation of the findings. While the questionnaire was a very comprehensive one, it is quite probable that some phases of family life were not brought out as completely as others in the replies. The policy, too, of obtaining the bulk of the information from wives and mothers with but one brief section from husbands and fathers, and none from the children, should be noted. There is the probability that other needs would appear if the opinions of several members of each family could have been secured. There is also the possibility that less prominence would then have been given to some that have been presented.

An additional point of no small importance in an evaluation of this particular study is that three-fourths of the women had chosen to take a college major in departments which dealt specifically with subjects related to the home. Approximately two-thirds of this group of home economics women were members of at least one of two national honorary fraternities in home economics which were helping to sponsor the study. Membership in either organization indicated qualities of scholarship, personality, and professional interest above the average of students in home economics. Because of these facts the group is an even more highly selected one than is apparent from the figures themselves.

There has been the intimation, if not the direct suggestion, from time to time that the present study was addressed to "successful" families. Approximately half of the group of coöperating women were selected as "the most successful homemaker of their acquaintance" by members of a professional fraternity in home economics. But, when one examines the term successful critically, one wonders if it does not lend itself to many interpretations by those making the selection. There is also the question of whether a successful homemaker can insure successful family life. Students in this field are still in need of a concise, acceptable, and easily applied definition to guide them in future investigations.

Thus far this chapter has dealt with the difficulties in making studies of family life and the weaknesses to be found in them. A seemingly destructive attitude has been presented for two reasons. In the first place, the writer has wished to emphasize the need for an exceedingly critical reading of the description and the findings which accompany the presentation of projects, regardless of how weighty and impressive the volume may be or how many tables may appear. A second reason is that since this is still the exploratory period of research in a very difficult field, those who finance, direct, or carry on projects need to be the more conscious of some of the pitfalls which exist. To make haste slowly but certainly, rather than to acquire masses of information which can often be secured only by unfair demands upon the heads of families, and sometimes with injury to them, seems the more scientific approach. Because many of the projects touch so intimately the relationships of the members, the training, the appreciations, the insight, and the personality of the research worker are exceedingly important.

The Range in Studies of the Family.—With the present widespread interest in studies of the family and with the promotion of courses in family relationships in elementary school, high school, and college—occasionally with only slightly less zeal than that of the reformer—a knowledge of the research that has contributed to fact or method is desirable. In the following paragraphs will be found a summary of the varied types of studies which have been reported.

The work of Frederick Le Play in the second half of the nineteenth century contained the beginnings of modern social science, if we accept the dictum of De Rousiers.[8] Searching about for a unit of social investigation, Le Play concluded that the family best served his purpose. He adopted as a formula, "place, work, and people," and with this as the basis he set about describing the conditions under which the working people of France lived. His monograph, *Les ouvriers europeens,* published in Paris in 1855, is one of the earliest and most renowned of his studies. His recognition of the need for a method of measurement which would promote objectivity and completeness brought about the use of the family budget, for to him the items on the debit and credit side of the family

[8] In "La Science Sociale," *Annals of The American Academy,* IV, 624-46.

ledger presented the basis for determining the nature of the family, and in turn of society.

While the emphasis which Le Play placed upon budgetary studies would seem to make him primarily an economist, his interest in finances was a means to an end—the more accurate description of society in terms of families. His attempt to define types of families and his later writings, in which he predicted the future of nations on the basis of the family types in the ascendency, has undoubtedly influenced many students of the present era. De Rousiers regards the classification adopted as less important than another might have proved:

The characteristics upon which he placed emphasis were not the *main characteristics*. For example, he distinguished three classes of families, *the patriarchal family, the stock family (la famille souche)* and *the unstable family,* basing the divisions according to the method by which families in each generation disposed of their property, rather than according to the education which they gave their children which is the essential function of the family.[9]

In another connection he suggests that the fallacy of Le Play's conclusions regarding the future growth and decline of nations was due to his dependence upon this classification in making his predictions.

In spite of the shortcomings of Le Play's deductions, the value of the inductive method had been demonstrated, and the use of the income and outgo of families to measure planes of living became an incentive to economists. Ernest Engel, an associate of Karl Marx, studied the cost of living of working men's families in Belgium; and somewhat later his laws of expenditure were formulated. The names of Chapin, More, and Byington are associated

[9] *Ibid.*, p. 643.

with some of the earliest cost of living studies in the United States. The Bureau of Labor Statistics has made both early and recent studies in this field and the development of the minimum quantity budget for health and decency represents one of the newer contributions. The United States Department of Agriculture, under the direction of E. L. Kirkpatrick, has undertaken extensives studies of rural standards of living and the findings are now available. From the earlier interest evinced by Le Play in the French working men's families as a means of describing the social order in France, the scope of similar studies has come to embrace a wide variety of types in many different countries. In addition to the purpose of description the method is one which is coming to be used to prove the need of larger incomes among different occupational groups and to promote advancing standards of living.

The anthropological or cultural approach has been used for the most part in making studies of the primitive family. In this field the work of Hobhouse, Wheeler, and Ginsberg,[10] Westermarck,[11] Malinowski,[12] Briffault,[13] Mead,[14] and others is well known. The recent study of "Middletown" by Robert and Helen Lynd employs this approach, plus that of the historical, in studying a contemporary American culture. For the student of the family the findings regarding life in a small American city include many of special interest.

The historical approach and method in studying the English and American family, together with the prim-

[10] *The Material Culture and Social Institutions of the Simpler Peoples.*
[11] *A History of Human Marriage.*
[12] *The Family among the Australian Aborigines.*
[13] *The Mothers.*
[14] *Coming of Age in Samoa* and *Growing up in New Guinea.*

itive family, have not been used more comprehensively than by George E. Howard in his standard three volume work entitled *A History of Matrimonial Institutions Chiefly in England and the United States.* Goodsell's *The Family as a Social and Educational Institution,* and Calhoun's *Social History of the American Family* are others in the historical group.

Among the studies which might be termed biological in their approach and chiefly statistical in their method are Galton's study of eminent men, Dublin's studies of vital statistics based in part upon the records of the Metropolitan Life Insurance Company, Pearl's studies of population, and Ogburn's research on "American Marriage." This latter, made up of facts other than biological data, belongs also in the group of sociological studies of interrelated phenomena.

The psychological approach to research in the family represents one of the newer trends. Nor is this strange when one considers that the science of psychology is still in its infancy. Flugel, in *The Psycho-Analytic Study of the Family,* has attempted to explain by means of Freudian concepts the relationships which develop within a family, but his data are not derived from concrete case studies, nor do his statements appear to be justified by other scientific methods. G. V. Hamilton, in *Research in Marriage* and Katherine B. Davis, in *Factors in the Sex Life of 2,200 Women* have undertaken to discover the psychic aspects of marriage and individual conduct which relate primarily to sex. The methods used, quite as much as the conclusions reached, are of interest to the student of research. With the problem child as the point of departure for her study of the home environment, Blanche Weill has recently contributed *The Behavior of*

Young Children of the Same Family to the knowledge of factors affecting the development of children.

In the group of sociological studies Floyd House[15] places Helen Bosanquet and Charles Horton Cooley as the earliest of those dealing primarily with the structure and the function of the family. In *The Family,* by Helen Bosanquet, there was an attempt to describe the process of interaction within the group and its effect upon the several members. In Cooley's *Social Organization* the family is cited as one of the three primary groups, and its place in the development of human nature is tersely stated.

Sorokin[16] suggests that the recent trend in sociological research is from the general to the particularistic type of investigation with considerable emphasis upon correlations. His classification of the researches dealing with the family follows:

A. Correlation between family and home and personality and behavior of the members.
  Ex: Breckinridge and Abbott, *The Delinquent Child and the Home*
  Healy, *The Individual Delinquent*
  Terman, *Genetic Studies of Genius*
B. Correlation of marital status with other factors.
  Ex: Ogburn, *American Marriage*
C. Correlation of factors influencing a modification of various family characteristics.
  Ex: Lichtenberger, *Divorce*
  Thomas and Znaniecki, *The Polish Peasant in Europe and America*
D. Correlation of factors affecting choice and marriage.
  Ex: Drachsler, *Intermarriage in New York City*

[15] In *The Range of Social Theory,* p. 140.
[16] In *Contemporary Sociological Theories,* pp. 712-18.

E. Correlation of factors responsible for the sex of individuals.

Ex.: Von Mayr, *Statistik und Gesellschaftsleben*

F. Correlation of factors affecting the fluctuations of the birth rate and fecundity of the different social classes.

Ex.: Thomas, *Social Aspects of the Business Cycle*
There is a variation in the use of the word correlation in the above classes and in the other examples which Sorokin gives. In a few, such as Ogburn's study of American marriage, the statistical method yields positive or negative coefficients of correlation for each of the factors studied; in others, such as *The Polish Peasant in Europe and America,* by Thomas and Znaniecki, the case study method furnishes facts regarding the problems of adjustment but without the precision of statistical measurement.

Among recent contributions in which the approach is primarily that of the student of law are the researches conducted under the auspices of the Russell Sage Foundation. They include *American Marriage Laws, Marriage and the State, Child Marriage,* and *Marriage Laws and Decisions in the United States.* At the present time there is in progress a "survey of the social and legal branches of family law, including marriage and divorce, birth control legislation, and the financial relationship between husband and wife" not only in the United States but also in other countries. Dean Young B. Smith, of the Law School of Columbia University, is the chairman of an advisory committee, consisting of sociologists and students of law, which is directing this extensive study. Its objectives are:

. . . to uncover the hidden areas of the law which are affecting the family of today and yet pass almost unnoticed in ordinary life. . . . The second objective of the study is to disclose to students of law the major bodies of pertinent social science material relating to the family, and to consider methods of using this material on judging rules of law.[17]

Research which has for its object the securing of facts regarding the division of labor in the modern home, the hours devoted to processes of the household by wives and mothers, and the amounts and types of equipment used, represents another of the more recent approaches. The study of the use of time by homemakers which has been promoted in various states by the Bureau of Home Economics of the United States Department of Agriculture, with its findings, is significant for many groups. Independent studies and coöperative projects are being developed in many of the land-grant colleges with funds made available by the passage of the Purnell Act in 1925.[18] Studies of the costs and efficiency of household equip-

[17] From an article in the *New York Times*, May 5, 1929.

[18] This Act reads as follows:
Be it enacted by the Senate and House of Representatives of the United States of America in Congress assembled, That for the more complete endowment and maintenance of agricultural experiment stations now established, or which may hereafter be established, in accordance with the Act of Congress approved March 2, 1887, there is hereby authorized to be appropriated in addition to the amounts now received by such agricultural experiment stations, the sum of $20,000 for the fiscal year ending June 30, 1926; $30,000 for the fiscal year ending June 30, 1927; $40,000 for the fiscal year ending June 30, 1928; $50,000 for the fiscal year ending June 30, 1929; $60,000 for the fiscal year ending June 30, 1930; and $60,000 for each fiscal year thereafter to be paid to each State and Territory; . . . The funds appropriated pursuant to this Act shall be applied only to paying the necessary experiments bearing directly on the production, manufacture, preparation, use, distribution, and marketing of agricultural products and including such scientific researches as have for their purpose the establishment and maintenance of a permanent and efficient agricultural industry, and such economic and sociological investigations as have for their purpose the development and improvement of the rural home and rural life, and for printing and disseminating the results of said researches.—68th Congress, Session II, Chap. 308, Section 1, *U. S. Statutes at Large*, Vol. 43, Part I, pp. 970-72.

ment are also under way in many educational institutions and in companies manufacturing equipment. Thus, the earlier economic studies are being enlarged to include not alone facts which can be recorded in terms of dollars and cents but in terms of effort and time as well. It is possible that the increased opportunities for economic independence of both single and married women may help to account for this new trend.

Still another type of investigation, which is still in its infancy, is that referred to as the study of successful homes or of successful family life. Such research includes the study conducted under the direction of the Bureau of Home Economics and the American Home Economics Association,[19] the study upon which the bulk of the present volume is based, and the study of Home Atmosphere undertaken by a sub-committee of the White House Conference on Child Health and Protection.[20]   Ernest R. Groves' study of successful marriage also belongs to this type. The significant element in such studies as these is the attempt to analyze the factors which promote success in family life. The difficulties that arise in making the initial selection of families and in the methods to be used are apparent to those who have attempted research in this field. Obviously these will need to be overcome before the results can be compared and before they may be regarded as meeting the requirement of the scientific method.

Present Needs and Trends in Research.—The range in studies of the family has been brought out in the preceding section. Of all subjects for social research none is

[19] For preliminary statements of the findings see "A Study of Successful Family Life," by Chase Going Woodhouse, in *Social Forces*, VIII, 516.

[20] See "A Study of Home Atmosphere," by Rachel Stutsman—a mimeographed report prepared for the National Council of Parent Education (1931).

more dependent upon a synthesis of plans and of results than is investigation of this universal form of human
association. To strike out boldly in one direction, regardless of the contributions which those in related fields have
to make, will limit the dimensions of the program and
the extent of the findings. The overlapping of the interests is indicated by Odum and Jocher.[21]

So varied are its aspects, so complex its relationships, and
so numerous its contacts—touching every phase of society—
that it would be quite impossible for a sociologist, an economist, an historian, a psychologist, or a specialist in any narrowly confined field to make a complete study of the family
or even of a family. There is probably not a discipline in the
social sciences that would not consider the family legitimate
for research in its own special field; and in more than one
instance will be found what may be termed overlapping fields
of interest. In a consideration of the need for coördination
of the social sciences no better example can be found. The
rise and development of the primitive family may well be
held by the anthropologist as his particular province, while
the social historian will be interested to trace its later growth
and ramifications. And the family today—its organization
and disorganization, its place and functions as a primary
group in the social structure, the individuals who compose
the family and their varying relationships one to another, the
factors entering into heredity, the vast number of economic
and legal problems involved, and a host of other aspects too
numerous to enumerate here—command the attention of the
economist, the sociologist, the psychologist, the biologist, and
the jurist.

One of the most far-reaching contributions which students in this field can make to the advancement of social
research consists in a demonstration of the practicability

[21] In *An Introduction to Social Research*, pp. 79-81.

of programs of research in which each science will be represented and from which there may come in time coördinated and comprehensive findings.

Le Play's early effort to describe the family in terms of clearly defined types suggests a contribution which studies in this field have made in the past and a still larger contribution which they may make in the future. An attitude occasioned by baffling complexity in viewing social phenomena may be eliminated through the possession of an ever increasing knowledge of the principles underlying human behavior and the processes arising from interaction. A more comprehensive analysis of types of families on the basis of their interrelations both within and beyond the home affords a challenge to the pioneering spirit. The extent of its value in enlarging our knowledge of human society cannot be anticipated. The degree to which the home and family offers a unit for measuring social change is noteworthy in consideration of ways and means of increasing concreteness and accuracy in describing human phenomena.

It is in the contribution to methods of research that studies in this field have already proved an asset. Data regarding costs and standards of living have grown out of the initiative of Le Play and Engel and have come to occupy a place of importance in the economic world. It is in budgetary studies that the statistical method has found fertile soil.

The case study is another of the recognized methods of research that has been promoted through the interest in the family. While there is a distinct difference between case work and the case study, it is probable that the records of agencies designed for service in family and child welfare have given an impetus to the use of this method.

Such studies as those of William Healy and of Cyril Burt might be cited in this connection.

The initiative that is being shown at the present time by those who wish to study the less tangible aspects of family life, and by those who are attempting to study the sexual relationships in marriage and the family, bids fair to yield information on methods which will and those which will not work.

Certainly there is no field of research in which the need for mastery of the human factor is greater than in studies of the family. The ultimate contribution that can be made to a knowledge of social phenomena will rest upon the skill with which the student surmounts the difficulties arising from the nature of his material. His own limitations become a further obstacle in attaining mastery. To predict unqualified success here is a supreme test of optimism or foolhardiness; to anticipate improved methods and techniques seems the wiser course.

The extent to which the dynamic factors of culture affect individuals and institutions is well indicated by Robert and Helen Lynd in *Middletown, A Study in Contemporary American Culture:*

We are coming to realize, moreover, that we today are probably living in one of the eras of greatest rapidity of change in the history of human institutions. New tools and techniques are being developed with stupendous celerity, while in the wake of these technical developments increasingly frequent and strong cultural waves sweep over us from without, drenching us with the material and non-material habits of other centers. In the face of such a situation it would be a serious defect to omit this developmental aspect from a study of contemporary life.[22]

[22] P. 5.

The problem that arises from attempting to see ourselves as others see us is a particularly difficult one in studies of the family, to which no one comes wholly free from opinions and biases. Clark Wissler, in his foreword to *Middletown,* comments on this point:

> To study ourselves as through the eye of an outsider is the basic difficulty in social science, and may be insurmountable. . . .[23]

In contemplating the proportions of the task ahead the words of Paul de Rousiers seem particularly appropriate:

> It is this (that every loyal effort that is guided by science brings, directly or indirectly, a useful result) which leads us to hope that all sincere and enlightened minds will aid us in the work we have undertaken of making a methodological study of social facts. It is a vast undertaking; it eludes us; it exceeds by far our strength, our time, our personal knowledge. We do not dream of playing the jealous custodian of a system—of taking out a patent on it; on the contrary, we ask all those who love the truth to unite their effort with ours.[24]

How shall one summarize the task of the student of the family? It is to bring to the interpretation of social phenomena the attitude of mind and the method of the scientist and to further the advancement of knowledge through a more thorough search for social constants, to give assistance in the development of adequate methods of study, to promote a more certain mastery of the human factor, and, finally, to develop a new appreciation of the progress which can result alone from coöperative effort.

[23] P. vi.
[24] Paul de Rousiers, "La science sociale," in *Annals of the American Academy,* IV, 646.

APPENDIX I

A Comparison of the Three Sub-Groups in the Study

A Comparison of the Three Sub-Groups in the Study on the Basis of the Type of Educational Training of the Women

	Those without College Degree		Those with Liberal Arts or other degree		Those with Home Econ.-4 yr. course		All Groups	
	No.	Per Cent	No.	Per Cent	No.	Per Cent	No.	Per Cent
Number in Group......	53	17.3	25	8.2	228	74.5	306	100.
Years since marriage								
Under 2............	..	....	..	....	7	3.1	7	2.2
2– 4..............	3	5.7	4	16.0	49	21.5	56	18.2
5– 7..............	12	22.7	5	20.0	77	33.7	94	30.6
8– 9..............	5	9.5	4	16.0	44	19.3	53	17.5
10–14..............	21	39.7	10	40.0	41	18.1	72	23.5
15–19..............	7	13.0	1	4.0	7	3.1	15	5.0
20–24..............	3	5.7	1	4.0	2	.8	6	2.0
Over 25............	2	3.7	..	....	..	....	2	.7
Not Given...........	..	....	..	....	1	.4	1	.3
Size of Income								
Under 1800..........	..	....	..	....	4	1.7	4	1.2
1800– 2500..........	15	28.4	2	8.0	55	24.1	72	23.5
2500– 3500..........	13	24.2	5	20.0	57	25.0	75	24.5
3500– 5000..........	9	16.7	9	36.0	68	29.8	86	28.1
5000– 7000..........	5	9.5	5	20.0	17	7.5	27	9.1
7000–10000..........	4	7.4	..	....	10	4.4	14	4.7
10000–over..........	1	1.8	3	12.0	5	2.2	9	2.7
Irregular–Uncertain ..	..	....	..	....	..	....	..	....
Not Given..........	6	11.4	1	4.0	12	5.3	19	6.2
Number of Children								
None..............	..	....	..	....	..	....	..	....
1.................	17	40.0	7	28.0	91	39.8	115	37.5
2.................	15	28.4	11	44.0	74	32.9	100	32.5
3.................	17	40.0	4	16.0	50	21.7	71	23.2
4 or more..........	4	7.6	3	12.0	13	5.6	20	6.8
Location of Homes								
Urban.............	49	92.4	25	100.0	202	88.6	276	90.2
Rural.............	4	7.6	..	....	26	11.4	30	9.8
Women in Employment								
None.............	45	85.0	20	80.0	187	81.9	252	81.8
Part-time..........	6	11.3	4	16.0	34	15.	44	15.0
Full-time..........	2	3.7	1	4.0	7	3.1	10	3.2

APPENDIX II

A Study of Home Management in Relation to Child Development*

A Joint Project of the American Home Economics Association and the Two Honor Home Economics Fraternities Omicron Nu and Phi Upsilon Omicron

THE STUDY

Outline I Introduction
Information Blank

Outline II The managerial responsibilities which have to do principally with the provisions for the physical needs of the family

1. Provision of adequate food
2. Provision of adequate clothing
3. Budgeting finances and keeping household accounts
4. Provision of adequate dwelling
5. Provision of adequate equipment and furnishings

Outline III The managerial responsibilities which have to do chiefly with the family's activities and its personnel

* This questionnaire was sent out in three sections. The returns are indicated in the following tabulation:

	No.	Per Cent
Outline I (sent to entire alumnae and honorary membership of Omicron Nu and Phi Upsilon Omicron)	3,560	
Replies received to Outline I	939	26.
Replies to Outline II	590	17.
Replies to Outline III	306	9.

If percentages are based upon the number returning Outline I, the following is a summary of replies:

	No.	Per Cent
Replies to Outline I	939	100.
Replies to Outline II	590	62.
Replies to Outline III	306	31.

1. Providing for and scheduling home activities
2. Teaching and training
3. Coördinating family and community interests and activities
4. A section to be filled out if there are adolescent children
5. A general section
6. A section to be filled out by the father

OUTLINE NO. I

INTRODUCTION

This study is an attempt to clarify some of the more important home management problems, which are vitally concerned with the development of children in the home, by drawing upon the experience and the practices of a group of well trained homemakers.

The successful home must be run according to accepted principles of good management. These are not identical with principles of industrial or business management, as the objectives, for the enterprise are not the same. There are, however, certain parallels between the problems which the home and industry present and some of the principles evolved for good industrial management have significance for the home manager. Human satisfactions and development, rather than increased production or sales, is our chief aim. The training and personnel factors must, therefore, receive especial emphasis in any study of home management.

Function of the Home: As the home is primarily a social institution, the demands made upon it reflect the life of which it is an integral part and its functions are modified by the needs, thinking, feeling and the developing personalities which constitute its membership. In the main, however, we will agree that the chief function of the home, with children, is to provide an environment where the members of the family can live healthy, happy, useful lives. To achieve this function the home must (1) set for itself rather well defined objectives for the physical, emotional and intellectual development of its members and (2) must apply wise management in the handling of the resources at its command.

The Resources: The resources upon which the home may draw, are of two types, those furnished by the activities and personnel of the family, and those which the community makes available. The resources of the first type are the combined income, time, energy, personalities and special abilities of its members, as well as their good health, customs, traditions, knowledge, training and skill. The resources of the second type are modified by the community in which the home is located, but in general they are, schools, churches, libraries, hospitals, clinics, consultation centers, playgrounds, social, professional and philanthropic organizations, municipal services, public utilities and the racial and community standards, customs and traditions. This is a wider interpretation of resources than is often considered, yet the modern home must consider all of them for their effective use largely determines the quality of family life.

Good Management: Good management makes possible the accomplishment of the home's objectives through the wise use of its resources. "It is the correlation of the details of operation of an enterprise so that it will work as a harmonious whole towards the desired goal."*

The good home manager must first clearly see her objectives, second, she must organize the major responsibilities which must be carried out in achieving these objectives and, third, she must develop principles and methods for the use of the family's resources in the discharging of these responsibilities.

Although recognizing the importance of a number of different objectives for homemaking, this study is concerned primarily with the objective of all-round child development and

* Richard A. Lansburgh, Industrial Management.

the phases of management considered are those which deal directly with the accomplishment of this objective.

The following are some of the specific objectives for child development which the good home accepts for itself and to achieve which, it organizes its resources and its activities.

1. Physical Behavior
   To eat adequate food
   Take adequate play and exercise
   Good toilet habits
   Good posture and muscular control
   Sleep
   Dress self
   Bathe self
   Self help in controlling physical environment

2. Social Behavior
   Play happily with others
   Express self adequately
   Keep belongings in order
   Respect the property of others
   Assist with home activities
   Use money wisely
   Obey proper authority
   Good manners
   Coöperate with others
   Assume responsibility

3. Character Traits
   Share generously
   Tell the truth
   Build up ideals of right and wrong
   Stand by convictions
   Play fairly
   Ability to make friends
   Loyalty to ideals
   Respect for authority and for age
   Face reality

Persevere to completion
Consideration of others

4. Religious Ideals
   Use of prayer
   Relationship to God
   Service to man

5. Intellectual Tastes
   Pleasure in good literature
   Pleasure in the arts
   Creative work and play

The maintenance of a home where these objectives can be realized involves the planning, organization and the discharge of many important activities.

The following is a general classification of the most important of the homemaking responsibilities:

1. Provision of adequate food
2. Provision of adequate clothing
3. Scheduling home activities—work, play and social life
4. Budgeting family finances and keeping household accounts
5. Providing adequate dwelling
6. Provision of adequate furnishings and equipment
7. Maintaining health, physical and mental
8. Training and teaching
9. Character and moral development
10. Maintaining order and discipline
11. Recognition of special abilities, preferences and limitations of members of the family
12. Providing recreation and social activities
13. Development of right family appreciations and loyalties
14. Coördinating the family and the community interests and activities

Although there is much desirable overlapping, we can group these responsibilities into two classes, those which have to do principally with the satisfaction of the physical needs of the family, and those which have to do more directly with the personal elements, the less tangible, social, spiritual, emotional problems of family life. Under the first class may be included:

1. Provision of adequate food
2. Provision of adequate clothing
3. Budgeting finances and keeping household accounts
4. Provision of adequate dwelling
5. Provision of adequate equipment and furnishings

In the second we may group the responsibilities as follows:

1. Providing for and scheduling home activities
2. Teaching and training
3. Coördinating family and community interests and activities

Under each of the above there should be ways and means suggested as to the best methods used in accomplishing them.

Here we have little to draw upon, as few scientific studies have been made in this field. As many home conditions cannot and should not be standardized, our most valuable source of data is the study of a number of successfully managed homes. Your experience will offer effective help in the many important managerial responsibilities which homemaking entails.

Outline No. I   Schedule No. . . . . . .

INFORMATION BLANK

HOME MANAGEMENT IN RELATION TO CHILD DEVELOPMENT

A Joint Project of the American Home Economics Association and the Two Honor Home Economics Fraternities Omicron Nu and Phi Upsilon Omicron

Town   State   Date

I. The Family

   1. Occupation of father. . . . .
. . . .

2. Occupation of mother (If employed full or part
   time in some occupation other than homemaking.)

....

3. Number of years married........................
4. Nativity and main line of descent of father...........

....

5. Nativity and main line of descent of mother.........

....

6. Religious affiliations of father......................
7. Religious affiliations of mother......................
8. Education of father: High school?........What college degree?........
   What higher degree and specialization?.............
9. Education of mother: High school?........What college degree?........
   What higher degree and specialization?.............
10. Age of father..............
11. Age of mother............
12. Ages and sex of children:
    Age   Sex
    ....
    ....
    ....
    ....

13. List others living with the family. (Name relationship
    and indicate if financially dependent).............

....
....
....
....

14. Have you dependents outside the home?.......(Num-
    ber and relationship?.........................

....
....
....

15. Are the members of the family living close enough to visit frequently?........
    Name relationship ....
    ....
    ....
    ....
    ....

II. Dwelling

1. House..........Apartment..........Hotel..........
   Number of rooms..........
2. Does it have modern conveniences?..................
3. Does it have screened or railed porch which can serve as play space for children?..........................
4. Have you sufficient room in your home for your own and the children's privacy?.......................
5. Is there play space outside?..........Yard..........
   Farm..........Park..........
6. Describe play facilities:............................
   ....
   ....
   ....
   ....
7. Is there play space in the house?............Describe briefly:...
   ....
   ....
   ....
   ....
8. Approximate value of house?..............
9. Specify features of the dwelling which help to make management problems in the home easy: For illustration, a large attic for play space, an extra bathroom or spare bedroom, or anything which seems especially helpful to you.........................
   ....

....
....
....

10. Which make it difficult:........................

....
....
....

III. Help

1. Do you employ full time help?....................
2. Do you employ part time help?..........How many hours a week?..........
3. List kind of work done by household help............

....
....
....

4. What household tasks, if any, are cared for regularly by the father?..............................

....
....
....

5. With what occasional tasks is he likely to assist?

....
....
....
....

6. How does father assist with care, recreation or discipline of children?............................

....
....
....
....

7. How do other members of the family assist with household tasks or with the young children?............

....
....

....
....

    8. What special types of jobs are done by outside agencies?
       Laundry? .... Baking? ....Summer
       canning?..........Others?.....................

....
....

IV. Health
    1. Are the members of the family well?..........
    2. To what do you attribute their good health?..........

....
....
....
....

    3. What have you consciously done to keep them well?

....
....
....
....

    4. Have there been special health problems during the
       past two or three years which have caused anxiety?
       ....Taken much time?..........Required
       money? ....
    5. Describe briefly:.................................

....
....
....
....

     NAME...
     COLLEGE......................................
     YEAR OF GRADUATION.......................
     PRESENT ADDRESS..........................
Return to:
ANNA E. RICHARDSON,
617 Mills Building,
Washington, D. C.

OUTLINE NO. II

Outline No. II   Schedule No......

HOME MANAGEMENT IN RELATION TO CHILD DEVELOPMENT

A Joint Project of the American Home Economics Association
and the Home Economics Honor Fraternities Omicron Nu
and Phi Upsilon Omicron

Outline II covers the report of your managerial responsibilities which have to do principally with taking care of the physical needs of your family and include:

I. Provision of adequate food
II. Provision of adequate clothing
III. Budgeting finances and keeping household accounts
IV. Provision of adequate dwelling
V. Provision of adequate equipment and furnishings

Kindly fill out the attached using extra sheets where this is necessary, as full answers will be appreciated:

Return material to:

ANNA E. RICHARDSON,
American Home Economics Association,
617 Mills Building,
Washington, D. C.

MANAGEMENT PROBLEMS

I. The Provision of Food

1. How many meals a day do you serve?..........
2. Hours at which served?.........................
3. Do you prepare extra dishes for children?...........
4. Do you put up lunches extra?......How many?......
5. Are the school children at home for lunch?..........
6. Is father home for lunch?..........
7. What meals to the children eat with the family?
....
....
8. What provision is made for them if they do not eat
with family?..................................

....
....
....
....

9. At what hours do they eat? ....
....
....

10. Do they eat at table when guests are present? ....
11. Do you entertain guests occasionally? ....Frequently? ....Not at all? ....
12. What difference, if any, is made in meals when guests are present? ....
13. Tell some ways in which you simplify the food preparations for guests? ....
....
....
....
....

14. What are the plans you use which simplify or lessen the time in the preparation of extra dishes for the children's meals? ....
....
....
....
....

15. What are your most difficult problems in connection with feeding your children? ....
....
....
....
....

16. How do you solve them? ....
....
....
....
....

17. What are some of the food problems with which you need help? . . . .
. . . .
. . . .
. . . .
. . . .

18. Are markets adequate for your food needs? . . . .
19. Do you do your marketing largely by phone? . . . .
    At cash and carry? . . . . How else? . . . .
. . . .
. . . .

20. Tell ways in which you have simplified your marketing: . . . .
. . . .
. . . .
. . . .
. . . .

II. Provision of Clothing
1. What garments if any do you make regularly for the family? . . . .
. . . .
. . . .
. . . .

2. What garments if any do you make occasionally for the family? . . . .
. . . .
. . . .
. . . .

3. What do you mend? . . . .
. . . .
. . . .
. . . .
. . . .

4. What do you make over? . . . .
. . . .

. . . .
. . . .
. . . .

5. What household furnishings do you make? . . . .
. . . .
. . . .
. . . .
. . . .

6. Do you have your sewing done at home by paid help?
   Explain: . . . .
. . . .
. . . .
. . . .
. . . .

7. Do the older children take any part in making or
   mending of their clothing? Explain: . . . .
. . . .
. . . .
. . . .
. . . .

8. Do you do the buying for the family? . . . .
9. Do you buy for your husband? . . . . What gar-
   ments? . . . .
.   . . .
. . . .
. . . .

10. Do you keep a record of when you buy garments or
    materials? . . . .
11. Do you keep a check on the life time of clothing or
    furnishings? . . . .
12. How do you do this? . . . .
. . . .
. . . .
. . . .

13. What are the chief factors which affect your choice of
    clothing? . . . .

....
....
....

14. What are your most time consuming elements in the matter of shopping? Limited choice in stores? ....Demand for specialties?..........Limited clothing budget?..........Demand for unusual sizes?..........Lack of knowing in advance what you need?..........What you want?.......... Preference for unusual styles?..........Others?

....

15. What helps in shopping have you found most effective?
....
....
....

16. Do you give the children a chance to express their choice in the selection of their clothes?.......... Explain:...
....
....
....

17. What are the most important problems which you have to meet in providing clothes for the children?
....
....
....
....

18. How have you solved them?......................
....
....
....
....

19. What are the special problems in regard to providing clothing for the family with which you need help?
....
....

III. Budgeting Finances

    1. Check total income range: $ 1800 to $ 2500..........
                                    $ 2500 to $ 3500..........
                                    $ 3500 to $ 5000..........
                                    $ 5000 to $ 7000..........
                                    $ 7000 to $10000..........
                                    $10000 and over..........

    2. Do you budget your income?..........

    3. Is the budget made as a result of a family council?
....

    4. Upon what expenditures do the children have a voice, and at what age did they begin to take an interest?
....
....
....
....

    5. Do you have a food budget?.........Daily?.........
       Weekly? .... Monthly? .... Yearly?
....

    6. If you do not think this desirable, please explain:
....
....
....
....

    7. Do you have a clothing budget?..........
    8. To cover what period of time?..........Months?
....

    9. If you do not think this desirable, please explain:
....
....
....

    10. Do you have a detailed budget for recreation and social activities?..........Explain:..............
....
....
....

11. Do you have an educational budget?.........Explain:
....
....
....

12. Do you have a budget for household furnishings and
    equipment?...........To cover what period of
    time?.........Months?......................

13. If you do not think this desirable, please explain:
....
....
....
....

14. State briefly the general method of budgeting used for
    all household activities?........................
....
....
....
....

15. Are the children given an allowance?..........At
    what age did you start?.......................
....
....
....
....

16. Have they been able to get more than the allowance
    by asking you?..........Their father?..........

17. Are they paid for doing household tasks?..........
    State reasons for answer:.................... ....
....
....
....
....

18. Do the children earn money outside of the home?
    ....For what tasks?......................
....
....

. . . .
. . . .
. . . .

19. Are finances a source of worry?. . . . . Irritation?
. . . . Family discord?. . . . . Pleasant conference?. . . . .

20. What are your most difficult problems in connection
with budgeting finances?. . . . .
. . . .
. . . .
. . . .
. . . .

21. How are you solving them?. . . . .
. . . .
. . . .
. . . .
. . . .

22. What are the problems in regard to finances with
which you need help?. . . . .
. . . .
. . . .
. . . .
. . . .

IV. Housing

1. What were the chief considerations in choosing the
locality in which you live? Income?. . . . .
Business of Husband?. . . . . Of self?. . . . .
School facilities?. . . . . Neighbors?. . . . .
Amusement and entertainment?. . . . . Enough
space for children?. . . . . Accessibility of serv-
ice?. . . . . Health of some member of family?
. . . . Other?. . . . .
. . . .
. . . .
. . . .

2. What were the chief considerations in choosing your house or apartment? Income?.........Space for children?..........Light and air?..........Simplification of service?.........Neighbors?......... Health?..........Others? ....
....
....
....

3. What are the most important management problems which your present housing situation presents?
....
....
....

4. How do you meet them?..........................
....
....
....

V. Selecting Equipment and Furnishings

   1. What equipment has been particularly helpful in saving you time and energy?........................
   ....
   ....
   ....
   ....
   ....

   2. On what basis do you decide you can afford a special piece of equipment? (1) Cost?..........(2) Time saved?..........(3) Effort expended?.......... (4) Likes, dislikes and special aptitudes of family? ....Quality of result?..........(5) Other basis?..........

   3. Do you ever feel that for the sake of the educational value of the task for the children, it is better not to substitute a "labor saving" device?..........

   4. Explain answer:...................................

....

5. Cite an instance...

6. Do you find that good equipment does save you time
which you can devote to your children or to social
life?..........

7. Cite an instance.....................................

8. What are the factors that determine choice of new
furnishings?...................................

9. Are they selected with advice and counsel of family?
....

10. What furnishings or equipment have you purchased
principally for the pleasure or beauty which they
give? ....

11. Explain reason for selection?........................

. . . .
. . . .
. . . .

12. What furnishings or equipment have you purchased to
    satisfy vanity or a sense of keeping up with
    the neighbors? . . . .
. . . .
. . . .
. . . .
. . . .

                    NAME . . . .

Send reply to:
ANNA E. RICHARDSON,
617 Mills Building,
Washington, D. C.

OUTLINE NO. III

Outline No. III   Schedule No. . . . . .

A STUDY OF HOME MANAGEMENT IN RELATION TO CHILD DEVELOPMENT

A Joint Project of the American Home Economics Association
and the two Honor Home Economics Fraternities, Omicron
Nu and Phi Upsilon Omicron

Outline III covers the report of your managerial responsibilities which have to do chiefly with the family's personnel
and its activities. It includes

    I. Providing for and scheduling home activities
   II. Teaching and training
 III. Coördinating family and community interests and
      activities
 IV. A section to be filled out if there are adolescent
      children
  V. A general section
 VI. A section to be filled out by the father

Please use additional sheets if they are needed, as full responses will be appreciated.

Fill out and return promptly to:

ANNA E. RICHARDSON,
American Home Economics Association,
617 Mills Building,
Washington, D. C.

I. Provision for and the scheduling of home activities

In providing for the activities of the home we draw constantly upon the resources available both within the family and upon those furnished by the community. In filling out this section all resources must be considered. Because income is more tangible and because it is more frequently a comparatively fixed resource, it was discussed under a separate heading.

Unwise use of the family's resources limits its activities even more than does the absence of resources, therefore the home manager has a most essential part in family maintenance. Successful management demands both a knowledge of the resources at the command of the home and skill and judgment in their use.

The assets of the family are the combined resources as contributed by the individual members and are represented by their (1) Time (2) Effort (3) Income (4) Special likes, dislikes and aptitudes (5) Skill, knowledge and training (6) Family traditions, customs, standards (7) Health (8) Plant and equipment as well as (9) all of the wealth of resources furnished by the community.

In filling out this section, consider all of your resources.

1. Do you have a special plan for getting the work of the home done?..........

2. State approximate total amount of time which is spent daily or weekly, on the following activities and check under suitable columns whether you do it alone or with help.

	Time daily	Time weekly	Alone	With help
Prepare meals	....	....	....	....
Wash dishes	....	....	....	....
Clean up kitchen	....	....	....	....
Care of equipment	....	....	....	....
Set table	....	....	....	....
Clear table	....	....	....	....
Make beds	....	....	....	....
Care for bath room	....	....	....	....
Clean house	....	....	....	....
Do laundry	....	....	....	....
Iron	....	....	....	....
Bathe children	....	....	....	....
Take children to toilet	....	....	....	....
Dress children	....	....	....	....
Dress self	....	....	....	....
Hunt for things	....	....	....	....
Play with children	....	....	....	....
Read to children	....	....	....	....
Rest	....	....	....	....
Mend	....	....	....	....
Make garments	....	....	....	....
Ordering	....	....	....	....
Entertain guests	....	....	....	....
Outside activities	....	....	....	....
Other activities (Please list)				

3. Do you give your assistants a plan of work to go by?
....

4. Written instructions?..........
5. Do you do this for the members of the family?........
6. Does participation in outside activities make it more
   necessary to follow a schedule?..........or more
   difficult to do so?..........

7. Why?...

....

....

....

8. What plan of organization of your work brings the best coöperation on the part of your helpers?

....

....

....

....

9. What short cuts have you found most helpful in making for yourself a day of reasonable length?

....

....

....

....

10. How do you provide in your work plans, for interruptions such as callers, telephone calls, unexpected demands from some member of the family?..........

....

....

....

....

11. How does occasional sickness affect your plans?......

....

....

....

12. What are other conditions which make it difficult to carry out your plan?............................

....

....

....

....

13. Which of the family resources do you give the most

weight when scheduling the home's activities? (1)
Income?..........(2)..........Amount of effort
to do task?........(3) Time consumed?........
(4) Special likes, dislikes and aptitudes of members
of the family?..........(5) Others?..........

....
....
....
....

14. Which seems most necessary to consider in getting
    things done well and with satisfaction?..........
....
....
....
....

15. Which seems most important in getting the help of
    the members of the family?.....................
....
....

16. What are the activities which are your chief sources of
    worry?...
....
....
....

17. What are the activities which are your chief source of
    fatigue?
....
....
....
....

18. What are the activities which cause the most friction?
....
....
....

19. What plan have you used to eliminate any of these?

....

....

....

20. For the sake of training, do you ever let your children
    help even though it does take more time and effort
    on your part?..........
21. Cite instances......................................

....

....

....

....

22. Do the children have regular tasks about the house or
    garden?..........
    What are they?....................................

....

....

....

....

23. Do you feel it is advisable for the mother to be relieved
    of the care of her young children for some time
    each day?..........
24. State reasons:....................................

....

....

....

....

25. What are the most effective means you have found to
    meet this need?............................

....

....

....

....

26. What is your plan for the recreational activities of the
    family?..

....

....
.. ..
....

27. What are the most enjoyable and successful forms of family recreation?............................
....
....
....
....

28. What part do the children take in social or recreational life?...
....
....
....
....

29. Do they assist in making the plans?.................
....
....
....
....

30. Do your children make friends easily with their own sex?...........With the opposite sex?..........
31. Do the children's friends come to the home?..........
32. Do you have a victrola?.........Radio?..........
Piano?........Other musical instruments?........
33. Do you read aloud to children?..........To husband?
....
34. How do you usually spend the summer vacation?.....
....
....
....

35. What special customs are observed in regard to Christmas, Thanksgiving, or Birthdays?................
....
....

. . . .
. . . .

36. How do the children love best to spend a holiday or a
    special recreation period? . . . .
. . . .
. . . .
. . . .
. . . .

37. What do they regard as a special treat? . . . .
. . . .
. . . .
. . . .

38. What is your best plan for finding leisure for recreation
    or interrupted time with your children or husband?
. . . .
. . . .
. . . .
. . . .

II. Teaching and Training

Although the development of these habits, traits, ideals and tastes, is one of the main objectives of our homemaking and have therefore been considered throughout, they are so important that they deserve to be taken up under "teaching responsibilities" for the home.

  1. List your most effective methods in providing opportunities for the children to develop along the following lines:
     (Please use separate sheets, as full answers will be appreciated)
     As you may not feel that you can take the time to go into this section in the detail demanded, please choose either one problem under each of the five headings and write up quite fully, or give a few high points in your teaching program for as many of them as you can.

A. *Physical Behavior*

> To eat adequate food
> Take adequate play and exercise
> Good toilet habits
> Good posture and muscular control
> Sleep
> Dress self
> Bathe self

B. *Social Behavior*

> Play happily with others
> Express self adequately
> Keep belongings in order
> Respect the property of others
> Assist with home activities
> Use money wisely
> Obey proper authority
> Good manners
> Coöperation with others
> Assume responsibility

C. *Character Traits*

> Share generously
> Tell the truth
> Understand right and wrong
> Stand by convictions
> Play fairly
> Love associates
> Loyalty to ideals
> Respect for authority and age
> Face reality

D. *Religious Ideals*

> Use of prayer
> Relationship to God
> Service to man

E. *Intellectual Tastes*
     Pleasure in good literature
     Pleasure in fine arts
     Creative work and play

2. Do you think there is danger of the home giving the child too much guidance or supervision?..........

3. How can this be avoided?.........................
....
....
....
....
....

4. What are your most difficult problems of discipline?
... .
....
....
... .

5. How do you meet them? ....
....
....
....
....

6. List some of the most difficult management problems involved in providing environment where your child can develop the above habits, traits, ideals and taste...
....
....
....
....

7. How are you meeting them?.......................
....
....
....
....

8. With what ones do you need help? . . . .
. . . .
. . . .
. . . .
. . . .
. . . .

III. Coördinating Family and Community Interests and Activities

  1. What community factors make your homemaking problems difficult or complicated? . . . .
. . . .
. . . .
. . . .

  2. Have you kept up your interest in outside activities? . . . .

  3. With what? . . . .
. . . .
. . . .
. . . .
. . . .

  4. What community organizations are particularly helpful to the homemaker? . . . .
. . . .
. . . .
. . . .
. . . .

  5. What community resources have been of the most help to you? . . . .
. . . .
. . . .
. . . .
. . . .

  6. What community resources are most lacking? . . . .
. . . .
. . . .

....
....

7. Do you take an active interest in the school?..........
8. How do you manifest it?..........................
....
....
....
....

9. Do you and the family go to church regularly?........
   Some times?..........
10. How do you handle the problem of doing what "the
    crowd" does?................................
....
....
....
....

11. Have you a wide circle of friends?..........Few?
    ....Practically none?..........
12. Does the community stand back of projects for ad-
    vancement in education and social life?..........

IV. The Adolescent (Fill in if you have children of adolescent
    age)
    1. Do your children's friends come to the home?........
       Do you make any difference between their boy and
       girl friends?..........
    2. Explain:...
....
....
....
....

    3. What is the principal form of recreation for the chil-
       dren of this age?................................
....
....
....

4. Are there certain forms of recreation which you have forbidden at different ages?..........

5. Explain:...
....
....
....
....

6. How much supervision do you feel should be exercised over young people's parties?....................
....
....
....
....

7. Is community sentiment very conservative in matters of freedom for youth?..........................
....

8. Very liberal?......................................

9. Do family traditions, standards and loyalties help in maintaining standards of good conduct?..........

10. How can these be strengthened?...................
....
....
....

11. Do community standards and traditions help in maintaining conduct for young people of the type which you approve?................................

12. What community traditions make this difficult?.......
....

13. What opportunities do you consciously provide for your children to have contact with good books?.........
....
....
....
....

14. Worth while people?.............................

. . . .
. . . .
. . . .

15. Hearing good conversation? . . . .
. . . .
. . . .
. . . .

16. Travel? . . . .
. . . .
. . . .
. . . .

17. Other? . . . .
. . . .
. . . .
. . . .

18. Do your children of this age enjoy being together?
19. Do you spend much time in recreation with your children of this age? . . . .
How is it spent? . . . .
. . . .
. . . .
. . . .

20. What definite responsibilities in the home do your children of this age assume? . . . .
. . . .
. . . .

21. Were they assumed voluntarily? . . . .
22. How have you encouraged them? . . . .
. . . .
. . . .
. . . .

23. What responsibility for spending money do they have?

. . . .
. . . .
. . . .
. . . .

24. What responsibility for directing their own activities?
. . . .
. . . .
. . . .
. . . .

25. What are your most difficult problems with children of
this age?. . . . .
. . . .
. . . .
. . . .
. . . .

26. How are you meeting them?. . . . .
. . . .
. . . .
. . . .
. . . .

V. General
1. Have you held consciously an ideal as to what you
wished your home to be?. . . . .
2. Have you and your husband agreed in this?. . . . .
3. How much have you modified it as the result of experi-
ence?. . . . . .Explain:. . . . .
. . . .
. . . .
. . . .
. . . .

4. What have been your chief objectives for your home-
making?. . . . .
. . . .
. . . .
. . . .

5. Do you feel that you have paid too dear a price in achieving them?..........

6. What has been the greatest sacrifice you have had to make? Personal ambitions?..........A professional or other career?..........Chance to indulge special tastes or gifts?..........Individual freedom?..........

   Others?..

   ....
   ....
   ....

7. Have you held consciously an ideal of what you wished your children to be?..........

8. Have you and your husband agreed in this?..........

9. What have you done to direct their interests along these lines? ....

   ....
   ....
   ....
   ....

10. What do you believe is, ideally, father's share in the teaching and training of the child?...............

    ....
    ....
    ....
    ....

11. How much companionship, away from the children, do you have with your husband?.................

    ....
    ....
    ....

12. Does this make your problems more difficult?.........

13. What are the homemaking problems which cause you the greatest anxiety?...........................

    ....

. . . .
. . . .
. . . .

14. What have you done to solve them? . . . .
. . . .
. . . .
. . . .
. . . .

15. What do you consider your most important home-
making responsibility? . . . .
. . . .
. . . .
. . . .

16. What training is most needed to help you meet your
homemaking responsibilities?
More skill in household tasks? . . . . Economics?
. . . . Sociology? . . . . Psychology? . . . .
Nutrition? . . . . Art? . . . . General training in Philosophy and literature? . . . . Education? . . . . Management? . . . . Child training? . . . . Others? . . . .
. . . .
. . . .
. . . .

17. Could college have given you more or did the felt need
come only with experience? . . . .
. . . .
. . . .
. . . .
. . . .

18. What work in home economics has proven most help-
ful to you? . . . .
. . . .
. . . .
. . . .

. . . .
. . . .

19. What other college courses? . . . .
. . . .
. . . .
. . . .
. . . .

20. What are the most helpful stories, semi-technical or
    other material which you have lately read? . . . .
. . . .
. . . .
. . . .
. . . .

21. Have books or magazines been useful in helping you
    to get over a point to some member of the family?
. . . .

22. Explain what it was and for what purpose used? . . . . . .
. . . .
. . . .
. . . .
. . . .
. . . .

NAME . . . .
FRATERNITY . . . .

Return material to:
ANNA E. RICHARDSON,
American Home Economics Association,
617 Mills Building,
Washington, D. C.

VI. Fathers (Please ask father to fill out this section):
    We know that fathers do their part in sharing the respon-
sibilities of the homemaking enterprise and so we need and
want your help in this study.

1. What do you consider the most vital responsibility of
   the woman in the home?

A—Providing adequate food?..........
B—Providing adequate clothing?..........
C—Scheduling home activities?..........
D—Budgeting finances?..........
E—Selecting equipment and furnishings?..........
F—Training and teachings?..........
Some others?....................................
....
....
....

2. What is your share in the management of the home?
....
....
....

3. Is this what you think it should be?..........
....
....
....

4. What is your attitude towards a household budget?
....
....
....

5. Is too much emphasis placed upon minor details in the home? ....
....
....
....

6. Will you list suggestions as to how better management in the home might be accomplished?..............
....
....
....
....
....
....

7. Under what conditions are you willing to have your
   wife employed, on a paying job, outside of the
   home? . . . .
   . . . .
   . . . .
   . . . .
   . . . .
   . . . .

8. In this event do you feel the husband should share more
   largely in the home duties? . . . .

9. What do you think is your share in the teaching of the
   children? . . . .
   . . . .
   . . . .
   . . . .
   . . . .
   . . . .

10. Do you think that you and your wife should agree in
    the way "child training" problems are handled?
    . . . .
    . . . .
    . . . .
    . . . .

11. How do you settle differences of opinion in these
    matters? . . . .
    . . . .
    . . . .
    . . . .
    . . . .

12. What is your attitude towards freedom for young
    people? . . . .
    . . . .
    . . . .
    . . . .
    . . . .

13. What is the most important problem, of homemaking,
    which home economics leaders should be studying?

....
....
....
....
....
....
....
....
....
....

         NAME...................................

SELECTED BIBLIOGRAPHY

CHAPTER I

Abel, Mary Hinman, *Successful Family Life on The Moderate Income*. Philadelphia, J. B. Lippincott Co., 1921.

Andrews, Benjamin R., *Economics of the Household*. New York, The Macmillan Co., 1923

Beard, Charles and Mary, *The Rise of American Civilization*, 2 vols. New York, The Macmillan Co., 1927.

Bureau of the Census, *Statistical Abstract of the Fourteenth Census*. Washington, Government Printing Office, 1920.

Chase, Stuart, *The Tragedy of Waste*. New York, The Macmillan Co., 1925.

Dublin, Louis I., *Health and Wealth*. New York, Harper and Bros., 1928.

Goodsell, Willystine, *A History of the Family as a Social and Educational Institution*. New York, The Macmillan Co., 1915.

————*Problems of the Family*. New York and London, The Century Co., 1928.

Groves, Ernest R., *Social Problems of the Family*. Philadelphia, J. B. Lippincott, 1927.

Groves, Ernest R., and Ogburn, Wm. F., *American Marriage and Family Relationships*. New York, Henry Holt and Co., 1928.

Hill, Joseph, *Women in Gainful Occupations 1870-1920. Census Monograph IX*. Washington, Govt. Printing Office, 1929.

King, W. I., *The National Income and Its Purchasing Power*. New York, National Bureau of Economic Research, Inc., 1930.

Kirkpatrick, Ellis L., *The Farmers' Standards of Living*. New York, The Century Co., 1929.

Lippmann, Walter, *A Preface to Morals*. New York, The Macmillan Co., 1929.

Ogburn, Wm. F., *Social Change with Respect to Culture and Original Nature*. New York, B. W. Huebsch, Inc., 1922.

CHAPTER II

King, W. I., *The National Income and Its Purchasing Power*. New York, National Bureau of Economic Research, Inc., 1930.

Lindquist, Ruth, *A Study of Home Management in Its Relation to Child Development*.

CHAPTER III

Brinton, Lillian Pearson, "An Unpublished Study on Keeping Time."

Kneeland, Hildegarde, "Is the Modern Housewife a Lady of Leisure?" *Survey Graphic*, LXII, 301-2.

CHAPTER V

King, W. I., *The National Income and Its Purchasing Power*. New York, National Bureau of Economic Research, Inc., 1930.

CHAPTER VI

Lindquist, Ruth, *A Study of Home Management in Its Relation to Child Development*.

Mead, Margaret, *Coming of Age in Samoa*. New York, W. Morrow and Company, 1928.

Tilson, Agnes, "An Unpublished Study of Trends in Home Economics as Shown by Catalog Offerings in 1914 and 1924."

CHAPTER VII

Bulletin of Purdue University, Vol. XXX, No. 7.

Bulletin of the University of Minnesota, Vol. XXXI, No. 28.

Bulletin of the University of Nebraska, Series XXXIV, No. 12.

Bulletin of the University of Wisconsin, Series No. 1583, Gen'l. Series No. 1357.

Iowa State College of Agriculture and Mechanic Arts, Official Pub., Vol., XXVII, No. 41.

Kansas State Agricultural College Bulletin, Vol. XIII, No. 4.

Michigan State College Bulletin, Vol. 22, No. 10.

The Ohio State University Bulletin, Vol. XXXIII, No. 15.

University of Illinois, Bulletin, Vol. XXVII, No. 27.

Richardson, Anna E., and Miller, Mabel Lawrence, *Child Development and Parental Education in Home Economics.* Baltimore, American Home Economics Assn., 1928.

Woodhouse, Chase Going, "A Study of Successful Family Life," *Social Forces,* VIII, 516.

CHAPTER X

BOOKS

Bosanquet, Helen, *The Family.* New York, The Macmillan Co., 1906.

Briffault, Robert, *The Mothers.* 3 vols. New York, The Macmillan Co., 1927.

Byington, Margaret F., *Homestead: The Households of a Mill Town.* New York, Charities Publication Com., 1910.

Calhoun, Arthur W., *Social History of the American Family.* 3 vols. Cleveland, The Arthur H. Clark Co., 1917-19.

Chapin, Robert Coit, *The Standard of Living Among Workingmen's Families in New York City.* New York, Charities Publication Com., 1909.

Cooley, Charles Horton, *Social Organization.* New York, Charles Scribner's Sons, 1909.

Davis, Katherine B., *Factors in the Sex Life of 2,200 Women.* New York, Harper and Bros., 1929.

Dublin, Louis I., *Health and Wealth.* New York, Harper and Bros., 1928.

Mortality Statistics of Insured Wage-earners and their Families. New York, Metropolitan Life Insurance Co., 1909.

Flugel, J. C., *A Psycho-Analytic Study of the Family.* New York, International Psycho-Analytical Press, 1921.

Goodsell, Willystine, *The Family as a Social and Educational Institution.* New York, The Macmillan Co., 1915.

Groves, Ernest R., and Ogburn, W. F., *American Marriage and Family Relationships*. New York, Henry Holt and Co., 1928.

Hall, F. S., and Brooke, E. W., *American Marriage Laws in their Social Aspects*. New York, Russell Sage Foundation, 1919.

Hamilton, G. V., *A Research in Marriage*. New York, A. and C. Boni, 1929.

Healy, Wm., et al., *Reconstructing Behavior in Youth*. New York, A. A. Knopf, 1929.

Hobhouse, L. T., Wheeler, G. C., and M. Ginsberg, *The Material Culture and Social Institutions of the Simpler Peoples*. London, Chapman and Hall, 1915.

House, Floyd, *The Range of Social Theory*. New York, Henry Holt and Co., 1929.

Howard, George E., *A History of Matrimonial Institutions*. 3 vols. Chicago, The University of Chicago Press, 1904.

Kirkpatrick, Ellis L., *The Farmers' Standards of Living*. New York. The Century Co., 1929.

Lynd, Robert S., and Lynd, Helen, *Middletown*. New York, Harcourt, Brace and Co., 1928.

Malinowski, B., *The Family Among the Australian Aborigines*. London, The University of London Press, 1913.

May, Geoffrey, *Marriage Laws and Decisions in the United States*. New York, Russell Sage Foundation, 1929.

Mead, Margaret, *Coming of Age in Samoa*. New York, W. Morrow and Co., 1928.

——— *Growing up in New Guinea*. New York, W. Morrow and Co., 1930.

More, L. T., *Wage Earners' Budgets*. New York, Henry Holt and Co., 1907.

Odum, H. W., and Jocher, Katharine, *An Introduction to Social Research*. New York, Henry Holt and Co., 1929.

Pearl, Raymond, *Studies in Human Biology*. Baltimore, Williams and Wilkins, 1924.

Richmond, Mary E., and Hall, F. S., *Child Marriage.* New York, Russell Sage Foundation, 1925. *Marriage and the State.* New York, Russell Sage Foundation, 1929.

Sorokin, P. A., *Contemporary Sociological Theories.* New York, Harper and Bros., 1928.

Thomas, W. I., and Znaniecki, F., *The Polish Peasant in Europe and America.* Chicago, The University of Chicago Press, 1918.

U. S. Bureau of Census, *Marriage and Divorce (1876-1906)* Washington, Govt. Printing Office, 1908-09.

Weill, Blanche, *The Behavior of Young Children of the Same Family.* Cambridge, Harvard University Press, 1927.

Westermarck, Edward, *A History of Human Marriage.* 3 vols. London, Macmillan Co., 1891.

ARTICLES AND REPORTS

De Rousiers, Paul, "La science sociale," *Annals of the American Academy of Political and Social Science,* IV, 620-46.

Jocher, Katharine, "Methods of Research in Studying the Family," *The Family,* IX, 85.

Stutsman, Rachel, *A Study of Home Atmosphere.* New York, National Council of Parent Education, 1931.

Woodhouse, Chase Going, "A Study of Successful Family Life," *Social Forces,* VIII, 516.

——— "Managing the Money in Successful Families," *Journal of Home Economics,* XXIII, 1-15.

INDEX

238 INDEX

ECONOMIC factors in relation to
family life, 4 ff.
Economic needs of families, 69 ff. *See*
Income.
Economic soundness, not entirely dependent on size of income, 56-58
Economics, courses in, 109-10, 133
Education, courses in, 109-10; of parents helps to determine that of children, 67-68
Educational agencies and the family,
141-43
Educational needs for marriage and
parenthood, 87 ff.; courses in art
and design, 94-95; in child development, 95-97; in foods and nutrition, 97-101; in health, 101; in
management, 102-4; in textiles and
clothing, 105-9. *See* Education.
Engel, Ernest, 179, 187
English, courses in, 110

*FACTORS in the Sex Life of 2,200
Women,* by Katherine B. Davis, 181
Factory system, effect of on family
life, 4, 7-9
Families in the group studied, amount
of education of parents in, 27; ages
of parents in, 28; number of years
established, 28; number of children in, 29; occupation of parents
in, 30; incomes of, 30-31; distribution of, 31
*Family as a Social and Educational In-
stitution,* by Goodsell, 181
Family, The, by Helen Bosanquet,
182
Family, the, variety in pattern of, 3-4,
25; change in size of, 21-22; range
of study of, 178 ff.; present needs
and trends in research of, 185 ff.;
complexity of, 186. *See* Scientific
study of the family.
Family life, queries for the student
of, 48-49; dependent upon physical
constitutions, 54-55; upon income,
55-58; upon parents' philosophies

of life, 58-60; on managerial ability
of homemakers, 60-61; on the
physical plant, 61-62; on housekeeping skills of wife and mother,
62-63; on abilities of members of
the household, 63-64; on personality traits of members, 64-65; on
the community, 65-68; need of
training for after leaving college,
139; and the community, 141 ff.;
healthful, definition of, 157
Farm ownership, decrease of in U. S.,
10
Father, share of in the work of the
home, 38. *See* Husband.
Fatigue, sources of, 34 ff.; caused by
direction of children, 36; by physical care of infants, 36; by being always on call, 36; by laundering, 37-
38; by sewing and mending, 38;
by care of house, 38; by dislike of
task, 38-39; by food preparation,
39; influenced by housing conditions and equipment, 39; by attempts to maintain high standards,
40; by length of working day, 40-
43; is it necessary, 50
Flugel, J. C., 181
Food, increased cost of, 82. *See* Diet.
Food buying, courses in, 122, 130
Food management, courses in, 122
Food preparation, courses in, 122, 130
Foods and nutrition, courses in, 97-
101. *See* Food; Diet.
France, study of family life in, 178 ff.
Friction, sources of, 45-48; caused
chiefly by overwork and fatigue,
45-46; by lack of privacy in home,
46-47; by lack of space in the
home, 47; by behavior of children,
47; by lack of agreement, 47; reduced by consistency and fairness,
166

GALTON, 181
Genetic Studies of Genius, by Terman, 182

THE UNIVERSITY OF NORTH CAROLINA
SOCIAL STUDY SERIES

Under the General Editorship of Howard W. Odum. Books Marked with *
Published in Coöperation with the Institute for Research in Social
Science.

www.ingramcontent.com/pod-product-compliance
Lightning Source LLC
Chambersburg PA
CBHW021813270326
41932CB00007B/162